LOVE AFFAIR WITH A CITY

Love Affair

with a City

THE STORY OF STANLEY M. ISAACS

BY *Edith S. Isaacs*

 RANDOM HOUSE   NEW YORK

THIS BOOK IS DEDICATED

TO MYRON AND CASEY—

MY NEAREST, DEAREST

AND SEVEREST CRITICS

ACKNOWLEDGMENTS

No biography of Stanley is complete without a word of appreciation to the people who meant so much to him, and who, through an overabundance of material, lack of space and the resulting "unkindest cuts of all," have disappeared from these pages: Arthur L. Strasser, Murray Bass and Walter Frank, his childhood friends; Ira S. Robbins, James Felt and Robert C. Weinberg, who worked with Stanley so effectively in the housing field, and George Naumberg on the Baron de Hirsch Fund; Helen Hall and Lillian D. Robbins, two of his closest associates in the neighborhood centers; Alec and Marian Mossman, Walter and Babbie Langsdorf and Jack Kaplan, among his staunchest supporters; Ruth Field and Trude Lash of the Citizens' Committee for Children; our growing family; his loyal political colleagues; and the hundreds of other dear friends who helped to make Stanley's life a good one.

I would like to include my special thanks to Casey, my daughter, who worked indefatigably with me to whip this book into shape. My thanks, too, to Rose Porter, Dorothy Brewster, Katharine Torrey, Betty Bernstein, Mary Perot Nichols, Millicent Sturm and Joan Hamlin Ellis, who spent many hours helping to select the most appropriate material from among the thousands of Stanley's papers.

INTRODUCTION

This book is not intended to be a biography of Stanley Isaacs. Rather, I would like, if possible, to let you know Stanley—the incorruptibility of the politician who belied the common conception of politicians, the unceasing energy of the public servant, the warmth and wisdom and selflessness of the man as a husband, a father, a friend.

Among other things, I would like to tell you how close we all were—Stanley, Myron, Casey, Joji (our houseman) and I.

As Joji often said about this or that, "Is too impossible."

But I can try.

CONTENTS

LOVE AFFAIR WITH A CITY

STANLEY, JOJI AND I

It would be romantic to say that our meeting was a case of love at first sight. But it wasn't. Stanley and I did not fall in love that steaming hot evening in July, 1900. We were meant to—an ex-beau of mine, Eddie Prince, had bicycled him over for the express purpose of fostering a romance. But we met on the steps in front of my house, where we sat silently and shyly until Eddie bicycled him home, disappointed in his failure at matchmaking.

We didn't set eyes on each other again until almost two years later. And then it was an accidental meeting in a streetcar on the way to college—Stanley was a junior at Columbia, I a freshman at Barnard.

Next came a phone call: Could he and Eddie come to see me? The answer was an enthusiastic yes, but why bring Eddie? He wasn't especially interesting to me any longer, and I didn't see why we needed a third person. But Stanley did, for the first few years, and Eddie was a most obliging chaperone. After a half-hour of talk he would complain of fatigue, yawn audibly and retire to a comfortable chair, where he would promptly fall asleep. This became the signal for Stanley to move hesitantly closer and hold my hand.

During the summer of 1904, Stanley stayed in Saranac, New York, nursing, cooking, caring for his eldest brother, Julien, who was desperately ill with tuberculosis. I stayed home in New York City, keeping in touch by mail. Our letters increased in frequency, length and fervor as the weeks went by, and when Stanley returned at the summer's end we spent a day together at the Edgemere beach on Long Island. Although he made quite clear what he felt for me, he didn't mention marriage, and I knew he wouldn't until he could support a family.

Stanley never did propose; the nearest he ever came was one day in 1908, when he asked suddenly, "When we're married, do you want to live in the city or the country?" I answered, "The city," and he replied, "That's what I want too."

After that Eddie didn't tag along when Stanley came to see me.

It was about a year later that Stanley told Minnie, his eldest sister, about our engagement. Minnie had mothered Stanley ever since he was seven years old, when Mrs. Isaacs had died, and I was very nervous about her reaction. "What did she say?" I asked, fearing the worst.

"She wasn't very surprised. I've always told her whom I was visiting, and it's been you most of the time."

Minnie and I met soon after that, and she couldn't have been kinder. A few weeks later Stanley invited me to a Friday-night dinner at his house, where we were to announce our engagement to the rest of the family. I must admit that I was more than a little scared, for I had heard much about the Isaacses—their importance in the community, their intelligence, their extraordinary achievements.

Stanley's grandfather was the Reverend Samuel M. Isaacs, who had been the rabbi of one of the oldest synagogues in New York and had read the Scriptures at the service when Lincoln's cortège passed through New York. Stanley's father, Judge Myer S. Isaacs, who died in 1904, had been one of the founders of the Educational Alliance, Mt. Sinai and Montefiore hospitals and many other institutions. Together with Theodore Roosevelt, then police commissioner, he was constantly making efforts to better the city.

Isaac S. Isaacs, the judge's brother, who survived him by one year, was an accomplished musician and an astute lawyer. Together the brothers established the well-respected law firm of M. S. and I. S. Isaacs.

The Isaacses of Stanley's generation were active in civic, educational and philanthropic affairs. Ph.D.'s, magna cum laudes, Phi Beta Kappas were the rule, not the exception. To add to this, it was a religious house-hold. On Friday night, the beginning of the Sabbath, no social engagement was allowed to interfere with the family ceremonial. And on the Sabbath itself, no travel-ing on streetcars or other conveyance was permitted and dietary laws were strictly observed.

My background was quite different in many ways. My grandfather had emigrated from Germany in 1848 and made his way as a merchant, invested his profits wisely in real estate and given his family of five the benefit of a private-school education. No Ph.D.'s, no magna cum laudes, for that generation. In fact no col-lege, and practically no religion.

I was somewhat of an exception, being a fairly good student, but even so, Stanley was disappointed that I didn't work harder at my studies and tried to encourage me, promising to buy my Phi Beta Kappa key if I was elected. Fortunately I had a faculty for boning up for exams. I would stay awake most of the night, drinking black coffee and reviewing my notes. The system seemed to work, and I managed to get elected. Of course Stanley was the first person I called.

"Have you got five dollars?" I asked.

"Yes, of course. What for?"

"Oh, just for a Phi Beta Kappa key," I said casually.

He was so pleased. "That's the nicest way of spending five dollars," he said.

But despite that key and all of Stanley's assurances, when I rang the bell at 110 East 73rd Street, I did it with some trepidation. The maid opened the door and ushered me into the living room, where the family was assembled. Minnie introduced me all around, without mentioning the fact that I would soon be one of them. Everyone was polite, but not particularly interested, and I clung to Minnie while the group continued the discussion that I had interrupted.

After about ten minutes of this, which seemed like an hour, Stanley arrived. When he kissed me there was a horrified silence. Stanley broke it with, "Well, what do you think of my bride-to-be?"

There was a great flurry of excitement—the family clustered around us, happy and chattering. They couldn't have been warmer or more welcoming.

Although my introduction to the clan was not exactly an unqualified success, I managed, in time, to live it down. At dinner I was seated next to Minnie, who was at the head of the table, while Stanley was seated far away at the foot. In an effort to make myself agreeable I launched forth on my most amusing anecdote and obviously was gaining the attention of everyone at the table, for they were all silent. Pleased with myself, I embroidered the story, and it went on and on and on. Stanley's head was bent and I noticed that he was shaking it. I couldn't imagine why. Finally a member of the family clinked his glass with a fork and said, "How about prayers now, all right?" I don't often blush, but this was a notable exception. I realized they had all been waiting through my interminable story to start the Friday-night services.

Later, when I came to know Stanley's family, I learned that Minnie, the eldest and most respected, in addition to her domestic responsibilities, was active in a variety of charitable organizations.

Alice, the head of the Botany Department at Hunter College, was a prime mover of Lenox Hill Neighborhood Association and Northrop Memorial Camp. At this juncture she was engaged to William C. Popper, one of the founders of the Educational Alliance and a solid citizen, a bit on the pompous side. I believe he made it a condition of the marriage that his spinster sister, Laura, live with them, and that no invitation excluding her ever be accepted. Laura was quite a person in her own right, but dinner parties are complicated when guests come in threes. Alice was a saint.

Next in age came Lewis, then head of M. S. & I. S. Isaacs. A talented musician, he was one of the founders of the MacDowell Colony in Peterborough, New Hampshire, where writers, artists and musicians are provided with individual cabins for uninterrupted work. His wife, Edith Rich Isaacs, a most intelligent woman with a magnetic personality, later published and edited *Theatre Arts* magazine, which flourished for many years. One could always be sure of meeting the people who were making news in the theater and the related arts at their "at homes."

Estelle, who would have shone in any ordinary milieu, was the least attractive, the least sparkling of the brood, but one of the kindest and wisest people I've known. She had been a teacher before her happy marriage to Adam Frank, a lawyer whose chief interest, outside his family and law practice, was a cemetery where much of the family fortune lies buried.

Isabel Isaacs, whose mother died in childbirth, was taken with her father, I. S. Isaacs, into the Judge's home, where she was brought up as one of the children. She was a pure delight to look at and to be with. Her husband, Edgar A. Levy, was a prosperous real-estate operator and an artist of considerable talent.

That was the family group I invaded. Julien, whom they all talked of with the deepest affection, admiration, almost reverence, had died in 1906 at the age of thirty-two.

It wasn't until after I was married that I became aware of the many problems I would have to face.

I was the youngest in my family and was my mother's

favorite. After my father died, when I was ten, I shared her room, her confidence, and had more than a fair share of her love. Naturally I adored her. I don't think she ever scolded me. I could do no wrong. I would rush off to school (usually late) leaving my things in the greatest disorder, and come home to find them neatly put away. Yes, she spoiled me.

In our house no two clocks were ever the same, and the word "punctual" was not in our vocabulary, so one of the most difficult adjustments I had to make with Stanley was learning to be on time. It wasn't easy, but I soon realized that if my marriage was to be happy I had to reform. I worked at it, and after a year or two did pretty well. But there were a few miserable occasions when Stanley exploded, I wept and he apologized. His apologies were always delightful—they made up for his scoldings.

"I'm sorry I was so prompt," he would say contritely. "I didn't mean to be." Or "My watch must be fast. I'll set it back two hours and this will never happen again."

Then there was the matter of keeping accounts. Though Stanley's family was well off, he was brought up to be frugal. As a result he insisted that I keep orderly records of household and personal expenditures, and he gave me a book in which to do it. There was a page for every month, a line for every day, and a number of fine-sounding classifications under which to make entries: Salaries, Food, Household Supplies, Clothing, Gifts, Contributions, Miscellaneous.

I had never kept accounts, and although I wasn't extravagant I certainly was not methodical. I would forget to write down purchases at the end of the day, and except for large items paid by check, by far the biggest amounts went under Miscellaneous.

When, after I had agonized a year, Stanley asked me what I would like for a birthday present, I told him: "No more accounts."

He laughed. "They aren't much use the way you keep them anyway, so okay."

The kitchen presented its own problems. After our marriage I had to learn all the Jewish dietary laws and teach them to our maid, which wasn't easy for either of us. No meals with meat ever tasted right to my heathen palate. After five years of struggling, she announced that she was leaving, and I staged a revolt.

"When you go to a restaurant," I said to Stanley, "you eat buttered rolls with your meat, and whipped-cream desserts. But at home everything has to be kosher. I don't think it's fair to ask me to go through all that bother with another maid."

Stanley was silent. I could see that he was troubled. I relented. "If it means so much to you, I guess I could keep it up," I said nobly.

"I suppose it actually doesn't, or I'd go to kosher restaurants for lunch."

"You mean you really don't care?" I asked.

"Well, I do care, in a way. It's a family tradition that I accepted as a matter of course. But now that we're discussing it, I guess it's not very important to me personally. It's part of the Jewish way of life, like observing the holy days in synagogue. But as long as you stick to one or two rules, like having no pork or shellfish at the table, I'm willing to cancel out the rest." I kissed him.

ʃ Stanley, now an attorney with M. S. & I. S. Isaacs, found his days fairly filled with legal work, but his ever-increasing interest in politics, housing, charities, neighborhood centers—all somehow interrelated—occupied most of his spare time.

The neighborhood centers—or settlement houses, as they are also called—are community organizations geared to meet the needs of a neighborhood through a variety of classes or clubs. They operate individually in local matters but band together effectively in pressing for reforms in housing, welfare, civil rights or whatever the need. The earliest neighborhood center in New York City, the University Settlement, was established in 1886. The number increased steadily until now there are thirty-six settlements operating more than sixty centers, all affiliated with United Neighborhood Houses of New York City, Inc.

In the early days most of the groups were led by volunteers. Stanley, then in his teens, was one of these—chairman of a club of boys at the Educational Alliance, of which he later became a trustee and then president. Always interested in civics, it was natural that he should teach his group the essentials of good citizenship and the fundamentals of city, state and national government.

His activities brought him into close contact with John Lovejoy Elliott, director of Hudson Guild and first president of United Neighborhood Houses. Before long Stanley was drawn into U. N. H. as chairman of the Housing Committee. Soon after, he became president, an office he held for twenty-five years, and later, chairman of the board.

In retrospect Helen M. Harris, the executive director, had this to say: "Stanley *was* United Neighborhood Houses; you could not think of U. N. H. apart from him . . . he held uppermost in his concerns the well-being of settlement neighbors . . . His passion for social justice, for civil rights and liberties, swept us into many a good fight . . . for fair-housing practices that culminated in the Sharkey-Brown-Isaacs law; for ever-expanding day-care services; for decent relocation of residents before the bulldozer struck, insisting that all projects be delayed until the housing needs of those to be displaced were taken care of."

𝒮 Nothing could have been happier than Stanley's relations with our children. No matter how busy he was, hardly a day passed without a "children's hour." The time that he spent with them had a quality that made a great impression on them. Playful or serious, he gave them a sense of values by his own example and by the books he gave them to read.

Our first child, Myron, arrived in June, 1911—the good little boy of the story books, obedient, helpful, always an honor student. Helen, a year and a half younger, who picked up the nickname "Casey" early in life, was a mischievous, imaginative, delightful little imp.

One evening when Stanley came home he found her enthroned on cushions, wearing an old spangled evening dress of mine, a gold paper crown on her head, and holding a scepter that had once been a kitchen fork.

"I'm a princess," she announced proudly.

"You can't be a princess," said Stanley. "Princesses always have golden hair." Casey burst into tears. "But of course that's only in story books," Stanley went on hastily. "In real life they often have brown hair, don't they, Mother? I'm tired of golden-haired princesses anyway."

The joy that lit up that tear-stained little face! Stanley had waved his magic wand and she was a princess again.

When the United States became involved in the First World War, Stanley was eager to enlist in the Army. But I—selfishly—argued that younger men without dependent families should go first. I succeeded in persuading him, and so he volunteered his services as chairman of Local Draft Board 164. In selecting his assistants, he made it clear that no salaries would be paid for services rendered. Most important of his staff were Dr. Walter L. Niles and John H. Iselin, topnotchers in the medical and legal professions. Arthur W. Lamm, Ottilie Appel and I (after I had taken a course in stenography and typewriting) constituted his clerical staff, with numerous less regular assistants. Spacious headquarters in a brownstone house in the East Eighties were loaned for the duration by St. Ignatius Loyola Church. The cost of running Draft Board 164 was minimal, the lowest of any draft board in the state.

It was during this time that Stanley started an informal luncheon gathering consisting mostly of lawyers and judges, who met every Wednesday to exchange their views. The group snowballed rapidly to thirty, including men and women of various professions—anyone was free to bring a friend. There were young and old, of all shades of political beliefs, and they sat around the table, discussing city, state, national and world problems. Stanley held that this give-and-take kept people alive and open to new ideas. From time to time he made a point of bringing in a distinguished guest to speak on some special topic. The young people, particularly, were welcome. Stanley was eager to interest them in state affairs so that they, in due course, might take their place in the political arena.

The Isaacs lunches still continue—although now they are monthly affairs.

In 1918 Stanley resigned from the draft board to serve in Washington as a volunteer in the office of the Secretary of War. But back in New York when the war was over, he organized a gala dinner and ball at the Hotel Astor, to which all the veterans of Draft Board 164 plus wives or sweethearts were invited. Financed generously by noncombatant contributors, it was indeed gala, with a sumptuous dinner, songs written for the occasion, an eloquent speech by Judge Learned Hand, souvenirs for the veterans, and dancing till the dancers were exhausted. The band had to play "Home Sweet Home" three times before they were allowed to quit.

In 1919 Stanley's cousin Isabel persuaded him to give up law practice and become a partner in real estate with her husband, Edgar A. Levy. Stanley explained his reasons for the change in a letter written to eleven-year-old Myron in 1922.

July 10, 1922

Dear Myron:

I feel in the best of health, and hope to live for many years; but of course that is something which no one can foresee. If I should die before having had the opportunity to accomplish those purposes which I have set before me, I would want you to know and understand my ambitions, and to be able to comprehend the motives that have actuated me throughout my life.

I have been able to earn a very comfortable living from my profession; on the other hand, I could never look forward to relief from professional work. I have spent a fair amount of time in civic and charitable matters; but I could not afford to give up my work altogether and hold public office, had opportunity offered, as I was at all times dependent on my earnings for a living. When the war came, I wanted above all things to enter service—but I had saved so little that I could not do so because you and Helen and Mother would have been without adequate means of support.

Your Uncle Edgar asked me to join him. He had done so before, and I had refused, but this time I reconsidered and finally decided to accept his offer.

In the first place, I was promised the freedom to engage in outside work of a public nature and to render social service that I was always eager to give.

In the second place, I had the prospect of eventually having laid by sufficient on which to live—and of being free to devote myself wholly to social and civic service.

This last was decisive. I have felt and still feel that a man of independent means can render service of the utmost value to his community, far more than the man who is of necessity compelled to earn his own living. I want the freedom that financial independence alone can give me to serve in my own way, without considering anything other than the service.

I may not live long enough to achieve independence. I count on you to be "true to your stock" as Roosevelt put it; and to achieve and deserve the place in the community that your grandfather and your great-grandfather held. And I know that you will watch over and care for your mother and sister if I am no longer here to do so.

> Your loving
>
> Daddy

Stanley's extracurricular activities increased from year to year, till finally he was on the board of twenty-three organizations. This involved much more than lending his name, for Stanley would never allow himself to be enlisted in a cause he didn't believe in.

Stanley represented his firm on the Real Estate Board of New York. Its members were largely conservative, and Stanley's attacks on the old-law tenements were considered revolutionary. However, he had the support of the liberal realtors and of many progressive organizations. In his capacity as chairman of the Housing Committee of United Neighborhood Houses, he wrote the following letter as the first gun in the Battle of the Slums:

November 26, 1929

Hon. Peter Grimm

Dear Peter:

The Housing Committee of United Neighborhood Houses, of which I am Chairman, intends to introduce the five following bills in the next session of the Legislature:

1 A bill intended to provide sufficient fire protection in the halls of old-law tenements to permit reasonable time for escape in case of fire.

2 A bill intended to abolish the dangerous vertical-ladder fire escapes, which give no adequate egress.

3 A bill providing that by 1935 rooms which contain no windows opening directly to the outer air shall no longer be occupied for living purposes.

4 A bill providing that in every old-law tenement, there shall be at least one toilet for every family, located on the same floor as that on which the apartment is situated.

5 A bill prohibiting the occupancy for living purposes of cellar apartments.

We expect to have strong backing from many civic and social organizations . . .

They are so sound and, I believe, so reasonable from a civic viewpoint that I think they should have the support, and certainly should not have the opposition, of a group of real-estate interests as representative and broad-minded as the Real Estate Board . . .

Could you arrange some time at your convenience for a meeting between yourself, myself, and Mr. Murdock, and anyone else who you think should be included, so that I can explain our program more in detail and try to enlist your active interest in it. I hope that you can arrange this in the near future.

With sincere personal regards, believe me,

Very truly yours,
Stanley M. Isaacs

The meeting was held, and through the years Stanley had the fullest co-operation from Peter Grimm, Alexander M. Bing and Robert E. Simon, all leading real-estate operators, in putting through his housing legislation.

Three of the bills passed without too much opposition. But hostility developed against the other two, and it took four years of campaigning: letters to influential realtors, to assemblymen, senators and governors, trips to Albany, before the last bill was made into law. I was an inconspicuous member of one of the delegations to the State Legislature.

Hiking, mountain climbing and tennis were Stanley's chief outdoor diversions, and hiking was the most important. He was seldom alone, for he had gathered into the warm circle of his enthusiasm not only his family but a number of friends as well. Babette and Walter Langsdorf, Anita and Joseph Despres, and the Fred Herz and Albert Heymann families were the regulars. Saturdays or Sundays and sometimes both, our gang and their children would join us on whatever expedition Stanley had planned: along the Palisades, on the Aqueduct, following trails or climbing hills in Bear Mountain Park.

Our phone was always busy on Friday evening. "Where are we going? Where do we meet? When do we start?" For Stanley always made his plans in advance. From the time Casey and Myron could toddle they came along.

Casey, the youngest, would keep going as long as she could, and then she would wail, "I want to be carried!" And Stanley would set her up on the top of the knapsack he always wore, lightly packed for hikes not too far from the city, and containing cooking equipment when campfire meals were scheduled. There she would sit in regal splendor, keeping time with a stick as we sang songs from Gilbert and Sullivan.

Stanley's all-day hikes around Manhattan (thirty-five miles), keeping as close to the shoreline as possible, were another kind of expedition. He took the first one alone on August 2, 1925, when he was forty-two. The children and I were in Maine for the summer and knew nothing about it until we got a letter:

I was on my own this weekend and devised the idea of following John H. Finley's stunt—hiking around Manhattan. I didn't dare tell you in advance, for you'd have fussed, and said I shouldn't, and that it was too much, and then, of course, if word had reached me in time, I wouldn't have gone.

It's a good game. You begin by going right to the river—East or Hudson, it doesn't matter—and start to walk around the island. You must keep right along the avenue nearest the river—and they shoot off quite unexpectedly. But if you go to the river too soon and find you're in a blind street, you go back to the avenue you started from, and lose strike and distance. And that *can* happen, as I discovered, until I became more cautious.

I took an early breakfast and left at 8:40 A.M.—*this* A.M. I teed off from the house* (I tried 90th Street but came back) over to East End Avenue, down through Carl Schurz Park—past numerous warehouses, Rockefeller Institute, model tenements, etc.— back to First, under Queensboro Bridge—then through Newport and Narragansett combined (Sutton Place)—tenements—slaughter houses—quite a

* Our home at 14 East 96th Street

mixture. Then I came to all the little "countries" on the Lower East Side. There's a little Holland, Bohemia, Poland, China, Italy—all complete in their one or two blocks, with costumes, customs, everything the way the people brought them from their own countries.

The letter goes on for six pages. A half-hour rest at the Battery, two orangeades and some chocolates, a conversation with a Mr. Hanson, a Great Lakes sea captain from Duluth. "Nice type," Stanley wrote. "He told me he had to have his tonsils out, and he didn't want to. 'I sing lots, all the time—voice like a nightingale.' I'd like to have heard him on his bridge sometime.

"It was fun, now that I've done it and don't have to do it again. Why travel abroad when you can see all the cultures of most foreign countries right in your own city—and see the city at its most interesting at the same time? I'm a little footsore, but not really weary, and I think for my years I displayed considerable forty-twod. (I'm glad I haven't had my next birthday yet, so that I could get that one off!) Feel fine now—rested already."

Though he wrote that he didn't "have to do it again," he did, three times more. Each time he led as many hikers as were willing to try it, and though groups of ten or more would start from our house, there were never more than three or four who finished with him.

In winter our group would go off on weekends to a hotel on Greenwood Lake, where we would skate, go sledding, play ice hockey, and in the evening play bridge or charades.

We spent many summers in the late teens and early twenties in Maine. I usually left town with the children in June, and Stanley joined us later. I'm afraid that, as a rule, my packing leaves much to be desired—by me, after I get there. One summer, when I was especially absent-minded, every letter I wrote to Stanley the first two weeks contained requests for him to send me things I had forgotten. After my third or fourth list I received this letter:

Dear Edith,

I have only one request to make—next time you leave for the country, take with you the things you forget, and leave behind the things you remember. It would be much easier for me. No wonder your trunks arrived so early—they must have floated up! Ah well, let me know if there's anything else you want, though there's little left here except a few mice in the kitchen, which I can forward if you want them . . .

♫ Eventually I found a cure for my absent-mindedness—at least a partial cure. It took many years and thousands of miles of traveling to bring Joji Kihara, Stanley and me together, but once we met, in 1944, only death could separate us permanently. Joji was born in

Hawaii, lived in Japan, Argentina, England, on the high seas as a seaman, in Connecticut, and finally came to New York to look for work. He was on his way past our house to take a job he had just accepted, when he ran into an old friend, Rio. Rio was our servant, with whom we had just come to an amicable agreement, the substance of which was that he was to leave; taking care of a large house was too much for him. He brought Joji in and made the introductions.

"I wish you take this job here," said Rio. "Is nice place, nice people."

"If place is so nice, why you don't stay?" asked Joji, reasonably enough.

"I don't cook good enough. Can't wait on table."

"My job right down this block. I come here teach you."

"No good," said Rio. "Me, I never learn."

"But I *promise* other lady. I can't do this."

Joji was about to leave when Stanley arrived, kissed me, shook Joji's hand and said a few words to him. Joji's eyes followed him as he walked away. "I take this place," he said firmly.

What was Stanley's magic? I don't know, but it was always there and it prompted a cousin once to say, "I can talk my head off to a room full of people, and when Stanley walks in, they melt away from me and surround *him*."

I don't believe Joji ever regretted his decision. He accepted us as his family and his bosses, but there was little bossing for us to do. He took over. As for us, we all became devoted to him. He was houseman, cook, butler, gardener, chauffeur, and most important, friend. He was a part of the family as long as he lived.

THE DEMOCRATIC
REPUBLICAN

Stanley's training in politics began at sixteen, when he
accompanied his brother Julien, a district captain, on his
rounds. Soon he was ringing doorbells by himself, getting the Republicans out to register and vote.

Through his father's close association with Theodore
Roosevelt, then police commissioner of New York City,

Stanley was brought up with a veneration for that colorful personality, and this he transmitted to his children.

We had a delightful photograph of T. R. with a small granddaughter and decided that it would be nice to have him autograph it—still nicer if Myron, then about five, were to meet him. A request for an appointment was granted, and at the prescribed time Myron and I went to his suite in the *Metropolitan* magazine offices, where we were promptly ushered in.

Roosevelt took Myron on his knee, and after the usual amenities, said quite seriously, "You look like a very nice little boy. Be true to your stock, and you'll grow up to be a fine man."

A few days later, when Stanley and Myron were out walking, they saw a billboard advertising Barnum and Bailey Circus. In the center were pictures of clowns, bareback riders, trapeze artists, and in the corners, pictures of a variety of animals. Myron pointed to one and asked, "What's that animal, Daddy?"

"That's a rhinoceros," said Stanley.

"What tricks does he do in the circus?"

"He doesn't do any tricks. No one has ever been able to tame a rhinoceros."

"Nobody?"

"No."

"Not even Theodore Roosevelt?"

"No," said Stanley. "I don't believe he ever tried."

"If he *had* tried he could have," Myron said decisively.

♫ A Republican by heredity, Stanley only once left the party ranks, and that was to work for Theodore Roosevelt when he ran on the Progressive Party ticket. It was a difficult decision, but once made, he gave it all he had, and in his district he rolled up a whopping majority for T. R.

The Progressive Party collapsed in 1916, and Stanley went back to the fold, where he was promptly elected leader of his district. He remained a Republican throughout his career, but always a rather unorthodox Republican, fighting the reactionary wing of his party on every issue.

His real career as an important figure in New York City politics began one summer evening in 1937. We were at a dinner party in Croton when Stanley was called to the phone. He talked a long time and was unusually silent when he came back. Soon after dinner he made an excuse for us to leave. On the way home he told me that Kenneth Simpson had asked him to run for Borough President of Manhattan, with LaGuardia heading the ticket for a second term.

"Of course you said yes, didn't you?" I asked.

"No, I said I'd think about it. I wanted to talk it over with you."

"How could I possibly object? I think this is just marvelous! It will give you a chance to do some of the things you've wanted to see done in New York. You'll be able to run that office as it should be run."

"You've got me elected already!" Stanley laughed.

"Yes, of course I have."

"But I'm not sure I'm going to run. You and I have had a wonderful private life. If I'm elected, there won't be much privacy left for us any more. And campaigns are brutal. I can take it, but can you?"

"Of course I can. Call Kenneth and tell him you'll do it." He finally agreed and neither of us ever regretted it.

I accompanied him on his first campaigning tour. We rode in a big limousine and had a police car with a siren clearing the traffic.

"This is great!" I said.

"I don't like it," said Stanley. He spoke to the chauffeur. "Why do we have a siren?"

"We make better time that way, sir."

"This isn't an ambulance, and I'm not the Queen of England," said Stanley. At our first stop he spoke to the policeman. "I suppose you have orders to do this."

"Yes, sir, I have."

"Well, no more sirens," said Stanley.

"Sorry, sir, but orders is orders."

Stanley resented all such special privileges. He even gave one of the two cars assigned to the Borough President to his staff for their administrative use. And he never under any circumstances used his one car for anything but official business.

His strict adherence to the letter of the law became a family joke. During Prohibition, when it was illegal to sell or transport liquor, we had three and a half bottles of assorted prewar wines and whiskey. Before we moved from our apartment to our new house (seven blocks away) Stanley went down to the license bureau and got a permit to move those bottles!

🖋 A political campaign is one form of madness—at least so it seemed to me as I went through the first one with Stanley. He had to give an overwhelming number of speeches a day, and except on the rarest occasions, no one wants to listen to a thoughtful address.

As he wrote in a letter to our friends Natalie and Edward Davison: "You have to go slam-bang through every meeting, using superlatives, hastily sketching what a wonderful job the last administration has done, implying none too hazily that you yourself are the best man to continue that kind of work, and then rush off to the next meeting." The usual routine included two luncheons, two dinners and a half dozen meetings besides.

One night we attended a meeting of the Yorkville Chamber of Commerce where half the audience didn't like Stanley because they were Nazis and the other half because they were landlords whom Stanley had forced to spend money on their tenements. It was vociferous and not at all friendly, but as a matter of fact, Stanley enjoyed that meeting more than most. I didn't.

Meetings in Harlem were also lively. At one huge

rally, where we needed a bodyguard to force our way in, the band played gloriously as Stanley entered. The crowd was tremendously excited and then looked obviously downcast because they had thought it was the Mayor. I minded less when the band struck up five minutes later for a judicial candidate and a few minutes after that when the candidate for comptroller walked in. In each case the crowd got excited and then showed their disappointment so plainly, it was really funny.

Stanley had a splendid press. The *Times* called him "that rare type, a practical dreamer . . . Without disturbing the traffic or blowing his horn, he has been usefully occupied for quite a while." He won by a majority of over forty thousand in an election in which about five hundred thousand votes were cast.

⌀ Stanley's first three campaigns differed greatly from each other and from the ones that followed. For the first, the Borough Presidency, he shared headquarters, expenses and publicity with the other candidates on the Fusion ticket.

The second—when he ran for the Council without any party backing—was something else again. Our headquarters were in the Roosevelt Hotel. We had to build up an organization, devise all our literature, prepare publicity and raise funds. I look back on that campaign as the most exciting of all. It was there that Victor

Weingarten, then a struggling young reporter, came to us through our friend Rose Porter and did a topnotch publicity job for the munificent compensation of one hundred dollars.

Two years later, in 1943, we decided to cut our hotel costs by converting the first floor of our house on 96th Street into campaign headquarters, a practice we continued for his six successive campaigns. While Stanley was becoming a councilman another member of our family was taking an interest in politics. In 1945, when councilmanic terms were extended from two years to four, Joji made his political debut.

Joji and I each had our duties. As campaign manager, I was responsible for corralling and instructing volunteers, drafting letters to constituents, working with experts on newspaper articles and advertising, and after the election, writing letters of thanks to all who helped and inviting them to our victory cocktail party. Joji's job, as assistant campaign manager, was to provide and prepare food for the unpredictable numbers of workers, to assist with the stuffing, stamping and sealing of the thousands of pieces of mail which he subsequently took to the post office. He always greeted Stanley's victories with elation but without surprise, because I doubt whether it ever occurred to him that his boss might lose.

Fund raising was conducted primarily through the mail, by asking friends for contributions. Stanley set a top limit of two hundred dollars from a single contributor, later raised to three hundred. Any check in excess of the limit was returned with a polite letter of appreciation and the suggestion that a smaller amount would be most welcome. There was usually a deficit, which Stanley met as a matter of course. Once, however, through some miracle, there was a surplus of a few hundred dollars. Painstakingly Stanley figured out the exact proportion of every contribution to the whole, and from that, each person's share in the surplus, which he returned. This unheard-of procedure caused quite a sensation.

Joji, who always made an unsolicited contribution, refused to cash his check for $1.29; he kept it instead as a souvenir.

⌀ As soon as Stanley took office—January 1, 1938 —he conducted a survey of administrative and personnel procedure practiced in the past, and finding tremendous waste, he undertook to set things straight. There was a terrific overload of employees in municipal offices and what Stanley referred to as a "general laxity" in performance of duties, which he systematically corrected. From January 1, 1938, to June 30, 1939, 126 employees were either retired or asked to resign—without loss of their pension rights. For 143 positions that became vacant during this period, only 53 replacements were hired— well-qualified workers who were selected through Civil Service or, occasionally, transferred from other departments. The thirteen appointive positions in Stanley's

department were reduced to ten. However, a statistical recitation of the changes can scarcely do justice to an event which resembled the cleaning of the Augean stables.

The Borough President's administrative functions had consisted chiefly of the construction and repair of Manhattan's streets and the care of its sewers, public baths and comfort stations. But even these few duties were given little more than token attention by the Tammany Hall incumbents. As one indication of the negligence of previous Borough Presidents, when Stanley began making personal inspection tours, he was greeted with surprise at every stop. "Sir," a Lower East Side bath attendant told him, "you're the first Borough President I've ever laid eyes on in all the seventeen years I've been here."

The BP's office had been one of the most blatant examples of payroll padding and one of the most secure refuges for political deadwood in American history. But other positions were often just as bad. At the head of several divisions there were ten-thousand-dollar-a-year employees who came to the office only to pick up their checks on payday. After Stanley became Borough President these men were rather upset to find that suddenly there were no more checks to pick up.

Over eighty men had been attached to the office as laborers, and here again Stanley uncovered an area of waste. Those who appeared at all were occasionally used to run errands, open doors or brush the coats of the staff. Though much of the Borough President's work was concerned with engineering, that department was staffed with faithful ward heelers, most of whom knew as much about engineering as an elephant knows about a Meccano set. Letters were often not answered for two months; the files were in a state of chaos; work, if any, began slowly, at any time, as the staff straggled in from ten-thirty to noon.

Into this paradise for loafers Stanley began dropping his bombshells. He horrified his staff by telling them firmly that their office hours were from nine to five and suggesting that those who found them too long might do well to seek employment elsewhere. His white-collar "laborers" he assigned to work on the streets and sewers, and they quit almost to a man. A general exodus began— some leaving by request, others resenting the demands of this strange politician who insisted that the staff of a political office be a working staff. He cut the personnel of the correspondence department in half and saw to it that those who stayed answered letters—not in two months, but within twenty-four hours of their receipt.

Many corporation inspectors, he found, were simply names on the payroll; they never appeared for duty. Those he hired were competent. Pavements ripped open for utilities work were, to the happy surprise of New Yorkers, promptly repaired. The Republican Club leaders soon learned that it was useless to send their favorite sons to the Borough President's office to fill a vacancy, unless they were capable. Stanley inaugurated an austerity program, cutting all executive salaries, including his own, by 10 percent. With a much smaller staff, working an eight-hour day—but working—Stanley soon found the job could be done in five days a week instead of five and one half, and the office remained closed on Saturdays.

LaGuardia was skeptical of the efficiency of the Borough President's office under these drastic cutbacks. But at the beginning of 1939 he revised his opinion. He had bet Stanley that the West Side Drive extension couldn't possibly be finished until May of that year, and in January, Stanley came home triumphantly with his winnings—a nickel. The extension was opened four months ahead of time.

Gifts came flooding in from people who wanted jobs or favors. Stanley returned them promptly with firm but polite refusals. No matter how tempting the present and how innocent its purpose, he stuck by his code. But he always declined graciously. "I wish you to know that I am deeply appreciative of your thought," he began, typically, after receiving a case of wine for Thanksgiving, "but I just cannot accept it. I cannot let your generous instincts violate what I know to be a sound policy," Stanley explained.

∽ Another accomplishment of Stanley's term as Borough President was the removal of the sixty-two-year-old elevated structure over Sixth Avenue. This he arranged after a series of complicated negotiations and

the default of the original bidder. It had been thought that removal would cost the city millions of dollars. The ultimately successful bidder actually paid the city $40,000 for the privilege of removing the structure and selling the materials therefrom. A unique feature in the contract was a clause which prohibited exporting the steel as scrap metal. This, of course, was designed to prevent the use of Sixth Avenue "El" metal as munitions for enemy powers. Instead, most of the El material went, eventually, to a Pennsylvania steel company.*

Stanley was concerned with almost any issue involving public welfare, but if there was one problem that concerned him most, it was housing. His letters and speeches on the subject were numerous. On January 6, 1939, he wrote Mayor LaGuardia about the necessity of radically revising zoning and dwelling laws, because he felt the city was "criminally stupid in building today the slums of tomorrow." Sanitary conditions were adequate, he said, fire hazard was cut to a minimum and rooms were sufficiently large, but there was a grave problem which was not receiving attention: the danger of crowding the land and cutting out light and air, which was bound to result in the city's being "as ashamed of the multi-family houses we build today as we are now of the old-law tenement." Stanley's suggestion was to lower the maximums for coverage and height by 50 percent

---

* The disposition of the El material became news again in 1945, when the Bryant Chucking Grinder Company published an advertisement accusing the city of sending the scrap metal to Japan. Stanley's outraged letter brought a prompt retraction.

so that the city would *spread* values instead of concentrating them in some areas and ruining others. Private builders, he said, should be forced at least to approximate the standards applied to public housing.

Roads and transportation were another of his main concerns. When seventeen New Jersey bus corporations applied to the Interstate Commerce Commission for permits to operate in midtown Manhattan, Stanley said the permits must not be granted without consultation with New York City. In March 1939, writing to William Chanler, corporation counsel for the City of New York, he urged that "the Law Department take immediate steps to stop the granting of these permits by the Interstate Commerce Commission until the city is able to work out a comprehensive plan to cover the situation." Chanler took action, and Stanley's cause was won: the City Charter was revised so that bus companies from all over the country, who were beginning to move into the city, were stopped at West Side terminals and not allowed in the midtown area.

The following year, as chairman of a committee to handle the interstate bus problem, he was battling strenuous protests against banning buses from the center of Manhattan. Stanley promoted the ban, and at the same time, tried to organize a union terminal near each of the natural entrances: Holland Tunnel, Lincoln Tunnel and George Washington Bridge—again, despite loud cries of protest.

There was protest, too, against his plan to help out the

unlucky pedestrian who might get lost in the jumble of house numbers. Stanley proposed to make the numbering consistent throughout Manhattan, with the house numbers indicating the nearest streets. The building numbered 8300 would be at the northwest corner of 83rd Street at every avenue, and 1401 at the northeast corner of 14th Street. However, the proposal was defeated by conflicting interests, such as the high cost of new letterheads on stationery.

The East River Drive, then under construction, was Stanley's greatest engineering achievement. Robert Moses, among others, has been given credit for it, but these are the facts:

The previous administration had abandoned the project of extending the drive along the shore of the East River, because narrowing the river would make the current too strong for navigation. Shortly after being elected Borough President, before taking office, Stanley wrote to Lawrence Orton, then Secretary of the Mayor's Committee on City Planning. This was in late November 1937, when the board was considering a proposal to continue the East River Drive in the form of a tunnel. Stanley asked instead for: "a double-deck drive . . . roofed and landscaped but open to the river." This would avoid diverting traffic underground, away from the riverfront. "I do not know whether or not this is possible," he wrote, "but I should like to prevent hurried action by the Board of Estimate, which might finally adopt the tunnel plan if there is not a reasonable probability that some other plan might be preferable."

By giving the board his "reasonable probability" that the tunnel plan was not the most desirable, he succeeded in putting over his suggestion. Two years later, with the construction of the drive well under way, Stanley's plans were justified. The drive ran "way out in the river . . . built on concrete piles fifty or sixty feet from the shore line, some of them going down at least that distance to bedrock." Each section of the drive had been designed to enhance private property values (taxable by the city), protecting views of and access to the river. One of the original plans had been to funnel traffic inland from 53rd Street through an underpass to 58th, and from there, after more detours, eventually arrive at the Triborough Bridge. By eliminating the inland proposal, Stanley saved the city $1,000,000 in land purchases. He also saved the city money by his diligence. Stanley took weekly walks between 49th and 92nd streets, and as a result of these inspection tours the cost of building that section of the drive was $800,000 lower than the original estimate.

The acres of new land created by the drive were converted into areas of recreation—for example, at Bellevue Hospital. Because of the drive, Bellevue would now have parkland for patients and recreation facilities for the nurses and interns. And this was only one of the many side advantages brought by the new highway— neighborhood parks at the end of some of the streets, an esplanade along the river all the way from 63rd

Street to 125th, plus an increase in taxable value of the surrounding areas—not to mention the highway it-self. As Stanley said, "The most important thing was regaining the waterfront that we should never have lost."

Saving money for the city was typical of Stanley, as was spending it for the right purpose. In closing a letter about the East River Drive, he brought up another current financial problem, involving the education budget, and concluded: "Incidentally, I am disgusted with the bureaucrats there who think much more of the excessive salaries than they do about the children, and cheerfully drop the most important work as a sort of blackmail to force the retention of their salaries."

After the opening of the drive, to which he invited the residents along the riverfront, thanking them for their patience in enduring the noise and dust of the construction work, he received this note of appreciation: "I have occasionally heard of efficient city officials, but never before have I met one with manners."

Stanley was both—efficient and mannerly—and was constantly correcting any misuse of public office. As an "efficient city official," he was disturbed in the spring of 1941, when it came to his attention that there had been a drastic cut by the Welfare Department in its clothing distribution. Knowing that the Board of Estimate had voted the usual allowance, he suspected an irregularity in the administration of relief. He wrote a polite letter of inquiry to the Commissioner of Welfare but received an evasive reply, which Stanley followed with a more insistent query. This elicited a vitriolic communication from LaGuardia, quoting obscure figures in a disingenuous attempt to show that the cut had not been made—which only served to confirm Stanley's suspicion that the commissioner had in fact followed the Mayor's orders to make the cut. Stanley had learned in the meantime that the proper allowance had been restored, and wisely let the matter drop.

✒ Stanley's correspondence was not always on serious matters. One of the bright spots in his career was his constant feud with Borough President James Lyons of the Bronx, which afforded Stanley as much amusement as it did discomfort to Lyons.

March 16, 1939

Charles Haskell Levill, Esq.

Dear Fellow Manhattanite:

This is to acknowledge your letter of March 9th asking protection against the infiltration of Bronx propaganda which has as its objective the annexation of Marble Hill.

You and other good citizens of Marble Hill may rest assured that I will protect the territorial integrity of Manhattan and resist to the death any attempt at anschluss of Marble Hill with the Bronx. I realize that this is no mere border incident. What we have here is an effort to create by wholly artificial means "senti-ment" for the seizure of Marble Hill by the Bronx fatherland.

You and our other fellow Manhattanites living on the Marble Hill outpost of our cultured borough should know that I will neither surrender this historic territory to the Colossus of the North nor will I permit any umbrella-toting Chamberlain from Queens or Brooklyn to concede away Marble Hill in the spirit of "appeasement."

Our armed forces, I must frankly admit, are small, at present totaling one (1) patrolman assigned to the office of the Borough President of Manhattan. Never-theless, I am sure that Marble Hill will never hear the tramp, tramp, tramp of invaders' feet. Its terrain not only has historic beauty but also lends itself naturally to the construction of any defenses necessitated by this new interborough crisis. Furthermore, all Man-hattan will rise as one man to defend Marble Hill, which we regard as dearly as we do Times Square itself.

You and all Marble Hill residents should remain calm, although watchful. Have no fear of strange noises at night. The Lyons' roar is worse than his bite.

Yours for an intact Manhattan.

Faithfully,

Stanley M. Isaacs

cc: Hon. James C. Lyons

His interests ranged from Marble Hill and Times Square—and all of Manhattan—to every problem spot in the world. Without spreading his attention too thinly to be effective, he added his ideas to those of other statesmen who were working on a world-wide scale. Whenever he came across an interesting or controversial item written by an acquaintance, whether or not the subject directly concerned Manhattan, he would answer it.

April 20, 1948

Mr. Chester Bowles

Dear Mr. Bowles:

I read with great care, and then reread your article in the magazine section of the *New York Times* of April 18th—and am in complete agreement with it.

You have done what I have been trying to do; namely, pointed out the fundamental error of our present international as well as national program. We have not realized that the best way to oppose communist activities here is to live up to our democratic ideals, remedy conditions which run counter to them and improve living standards. Similarly, in our sound effort to prevent the expansion of the Russian system, we should recognize the needs of the submerged people of other nations and assist in improving their living conditions toward freedom from fear and from want. We may be confident that they will prefer our system to that of Soviet Russia, once they know that we are interested in their welfare and have ceased to ally ourselves with oppressive and corrupt rulers.

Your program is sound and practical—in fact, it is the only program that can possibly succeed. We have followed the opposite idea in China, sinking several billions of dollars in the effort to stem communism by supporting the present regime, and the result, which should have been anticipated, has been the steady expansion of communist influence. Your way is the only way to stop this unfortunate progress. I am glad you wrote the article.

Sincerely yours,

Stanley M. Isaacs

ℰ Notwithstanding the enormous improvements in Manhattan for which Stanley was responsible—the East River Drive, the Harlem River Drive, the West Side Highway extension, demolition of the Sixth Avenue El, the controversial garbage-disposal plant, new baths and comfort stations, modernized machinery for street-and-sewer maintenance, the New York City Information Center and countless less dramatic achievements—after four years in office he returned to the city over $1,250,-000 of unspent budgetary funds allotted to his office.

For almost everything he did in office Stanley won enthusiastic support from the men and women of both parties truly interested in good government. But for one thing he was savagely criticized, and he himself admitted that it was a political blunder.

One Friday evening in the fall of 1937—before the city elections—Stanley came out to Croton for the weekend. "I just met an interesting young man in the train," he said. "His name is Simon Gerson and he lives right down the road. He's very well informed, and I think you'd like him. Why not invite him and his wife for dinner sometime?"

I did, and the following Sunday they came for the day. Gerson was intelligent, witty, attractive but quite radical in his opinions. His wife was quiet and pleasant. Stanley and he did most of the talking, discussing people in politics, the city government and what was wrong with the world in general. When our guests left in the evening there was a cordial feeling on both sides. I didn't see or hear of them again until after the election.

Then one morning at breakfast Stanley said, "I think I'm going to give Si Gerson a job in my office. I talked about it to Paul Kern and he thought it was a good idea. Later he called me up and said he had mentioned it to LaGuardia, who had said, "Good, the Labor Party's been pressuring me for jobs. This'll get the boys off my neck.""

"I think it's a good idea," Stanley went on. "I'm a conservative, and most of the people around me are conservatives. He'll be a good leaven. Besides, I think he'll do a fine job."

"That's great!" I said enthusiastically.

"He's pretty far left, but I'm sure he's not a real Communist." He added thoughtfully, "I suppose the newspapers will jump on me."

"Then for heaven's sake, don't," I cried. "You've had a good press all through the campaign. Don't spoil it now."

"Well, it isn't definite yet."

No more was said for a week, and then one morning Stanley told me he had made the appointment. "There'll be a storm, sure, but it'll blow over. Anyway, it's done."

Was there a storm! The headlines screamed: "ISAACS APPOINTS COMMUNIST," "RED GETS CITY JOB," "COMMUNIST IN ISAACS' OFFICE."

The next day we met LaGuardia at a political dinner. I was looking very unhappy, and LaGuardia put his arm around me. "Cheer up," he said. "This won't last. It's nothing to what I got when I was in Washington. Remember, Stanley? You'll see. They'll find another victim, and Gerson will be forgotten."

How wrong can you be?

Tammany Hall, of course, was especially vocal, delighted with a chance to get even. Fanatical groups distributed pamphlets at church services, demanding Gerson's resignation, some insisting that Stanley too must go. Groups of women picketed our house with signs declaring: "OUST GERSON-ISAACS!" and "DOWN WITH THE REDS!" The Hearst newspapers and the New York *Sun* kept up a running barrage of criticism, and even the *Times*, the *Herald Tribune* and the *Post*—all of which had supported Stanley on everything else—expressed disapproval of the appointment. The state commander of the American Legion suggested that a force of "shock troops" storm the Borough President's office and remove Gerson bodily. Only the *Daily Worker*, and surprisingly, the *Daily News*, approved the appointment.

Although Gerson offered his resignation early in the fight, Stanley felt that as a matter of principle he should not accept it. At the same time, out of loyalty to the Republican Party, Stanley took on himself the entire responsibility for the appointment, never publicly mentioning LaGuardia's prior approval.

But as the 1941 election approached, it became obvious that there had been considerably more damage to his political future than Stanley had anticipated. One evening he came home white and shaken. I knew that something had gone seriously wrong.

"Fiorello called me to his office. It was filled with newspapermen. 'Stanley,' he said, 'I can make or break you, and if you persist in opposing me on the Townsend-Harris issue, it'll be *break!*' "

Townsend-Harris High School was one of the best rapid-advance schools of the time. For some reason LaGuardia had decided that it should be torn down. Stanley had opposed him at a Board of Estimate meeting —a rare thing for him to do. He almost always backed the Mayor.

Stanley went on: "If he had given me good reasons for wanting to discontinue the school I probably would have gone along with him. But that wasn't the issue—it's really Gerson. It was outrageous, threatening me in front of the boys! That's why he did it that way. He wants to get rid of me because he thinks the Gerson matter will hurt his chances of election."

The school was torn down—with Stanley dissenting.

A few weeks after the Mayor's threat to Stanley, Mrs. LaGuardia phoned and invited us to dinner. In the course of the evening Stanley said, "Listen, Fiorello, I deserve renomination for Borough President on my record."

"That's out," said LaGuardia, "but I have two judge-ships in mind for you—you can have your choice."

"I'm not interested in judgeships," Stanley said; and that was that. But still, despite LaGuardia's defection, Stanley supported him for re-election, because, as he said, "no one else could do the job as well."

The Gerson affair was in the minds of all of New York's political leaders, both those who feared that the repercussions might prevent Stanley's re-election, and those who hoped that they would. David Dubin-sky, in a statement which would seem strange to any but those accustomed to political double-talk said, "Isaacs is one of the best Borough Presidents New York has ever had . . . I shall not support him for re-elec-tion." The Fusion forces refused to back him.

The Citizens Union, which supported Stanley strongly in a letter sent to Republican district leaders, acknowledged that he had made a mistake but went on to say that in spite of that "he has given the borough an outstanding administration and served the best interests of the people of Manhattan and the city as a whole."

One evening, soon after the LaGuardia dinner, Stanley came home looking happier than he had for weeks. "I've had an inspiration," he said. "I want to run for the City Council. But I don't want you to say yes till you've thought about it. It'll be quite a comedown from the Borough Presidency, but I think I could do a job there."

I was jubilant at the idea.

"The Council would give me a forum," he went on. "I could fight there for the things I believe in. And with proportional representation I think I could be elected."

That was quite an understatement. With no party nomination whatsoever to support him, he came in second among the six candidates elected from Manhattan.

Charles C. Burlingham, a prominent New York lawyer and one of the city's most distinguished senior citizens, never sought public office for himself but was deeply involved in every campaign for good government. He was one of Stanley's staunchest supporters. Angered at LaGuardia's treatment of his friend and disgusted with his maneuverings for a Washington post, Burlingham urged Stanley to come out publicly against the Mayor. Stanley wrote back:

Dear C. C.:

I agree with everything that you say in your letter except that I think it would be bad taste for me when I am just leaving this administration for a less closely connected office to attack the Mayor—and that is what naturally your suggestion involves . . .

The situation will never be straightened out until LaGuardia is persuaded to drop everything else and center in New York or to quit New York altogether —I do not believe he will ever trust someone else with full powers to handle civilian defense problems here. It could be done of course—Major Huie would be ideal for the purpose, Bob Moses would be excellent and so would Kenneth Dayton. I could name a few dozen others, but I don't believe he would keep his hands off unless his own work is confined to Washington.

I want to wish you the happiest possible years to come in this muddled world of ours. It is fine to know someone who sees so clearly through today's fog.

Faithfully yours,

Stanley M. Isaacs

In the March 9, 1942, issue of *The New Republic,* George Britt commented on the Mayor's behavior:

Fiorello H. LaGuardia, the great mayor, unquestionably the most successful and the best mayor in New York's living memory, would be beaten by a quick knockout if he came up for re-election today. This opinion, put as a question to a fairly wide personal sampling of both enemies and friends of the Mayor's, has yielded not one single dissent . . .

Here then, since late October, has been a succession

of thunderstorms in the Mayor's behavior, alienating a city. The Mayor for eight years, publicly and privately, has conducted a government by tantrum. The trick is working no longer. The Mayor's old joking reference to himself as "a cool calm Nordic" is not the joke it used to be . . .

Borough President Stanley Isaacs of Manhattan was one of the most useful public servants, perhaps the all-time best borough president, in the city. But he had committed an act of political naïveté by appointing a Communist to his office and refusing to fire him—"the Gerson case." When the slate of his running mates was being made up for the last election, the Mayor permitted the dropping of Isaacs without lifting a finger in his defense—a surrender to his enemies which, in retrospect, appears as needless as it was costly. . . .

The Mayor's present position in local politics is a headache, and perhaps not primarily to himself. It is distressing to hundreds of thousands who have followed him devotedly. If his grip is weakened for any reason, it is their personal tragedy; above all it is the tragedy of New York and the dimming of a hope given to decent government in every city.

La Guardia will have only himself to blame, the least sturdy and mature elements in his own character, if he does not look squarely at himself as others see him, if he does not hear the pleading of his best friends, and reoccupy a position in harmony with his past.

3

HOMES, SWEET HOMES

Stanley and I were married in 1910. Our first home was
a seven-room apartment at 77 East 89th Street. It was
in a comfortable old-fashioned building with pleasant
rooms—enough of them so that when our two children
arrived, there was no need to move.

We spent summer vacations on Long Island, in the
Adirondacks and Maine. Wherever we went, Stanley

would find some house with a view that he'd fall in love with, and talk of buying. "How about that one?" and he would point to some dilapidated shack perched high up on a rock. I always dissuaded him.

One afternoon in 1923 Stanley came home from his real-estate office with a light of adventure in his eyes and asked, "How would you like to live in a house in New York?"

"If you mean one of these little antique wooden houses on East End Avenue you once showed me, the answer is, I wouldn't."

"No, that's not what I mean at all. I mean a house we'd build for ourselves—plan it the way we want it and have the fun of seeing it going up."

"That I think I would like," I said.

"Put on your hat and coat and I'll show you where it will be," he said eagerly.

We walked to 96th Street, and I had difficulty keeping up with the pace he set. There, next door to a corner apartment house owned by the real-estate company of which Stanley was then vice-president, was an empty lot. "We can have the land at a most reasonable price if we agree to build a house not more than sixty feet deep. We have to protect the light of the apartments next door. Twenty by sixty is big enough, don't you think? And we'd have a back yard twenty by forty."

"Twenty by sixty—why, that's enormous."

Suddenly I found myself as excited about it as Stanley. We would live in a house we'd planned ourselves—with all the closets and bathrooms I wanted! As soon as we came home I began to draw plans. I know now that my ideas for a house were the most impractical anyone ever put on paper, bathrooms wherever I wanted them, without any relation to the geography of the plumbing. What Stanley found the most amusing—and never forgot—was the dumbwaiter which, as I had it, would have come right up through the middle of our bedroom. Stanley's ideas were more sensible, and I learned to keep my mouth shut when he and Melville Nauheim, the architect, talked over plans.

We watched that house go up brick by brick, climbing up ladders before the stairs were built, getting in the way of the workmen. But it was our house, and it is still my home. What a thrill when it was finished and we moved in, in June 1924. It is something of a landmark, four stories high, built of dark, irregular bricks, with limestone trim, leaded-glass windows, random-width oak floors, and well-proportioned rooms. Except for the addition of a bedroom in one corner of our huge kitchen and the transformation of a third-floor bedroom into a kitchen, there have been no changes.

When Casey and Myron married and were living in homes of their own, we rented the two upper floors, which are occupied by a quartet of girls who find their own replacements as they marry or move to distant parts.

Occasionally, when they are tardy in paying the rent, I send them delicate reminders. One that Stanley liked best was a rhyme I wrote long after their March rent was due:

> *The Ides of March have come and gone,*
> *No wonder I repine,*
> *For Caesar's clothes were full of rents,*
> *But there are none in mine!*

It brought prompt results.

✐ We still went to the country for summer vacations, and I still had to talk Stanley out of buying some sway-backed Cape Cod or salt-box house. But I accepted that as a matter of course, and never really took it very seriously until one day in January 1930 he told me without warning that he had made a down payment on a house and fifty acres of land in Croton-on-Hudson. "It's a very small down payment," he said apologetically, "and you'll fall in love with it the minute you see it. It's a wonderful piece of land with a marvelous view. There's a brick house right on the road that we can sell, and it will help pay for the house that we'll build for ourselves."

The next day we took the train to Croton. We were met at the station by the real-estate agent, who drove us three and a half miles on a rough country road up a hill so steep that his car stalled. It was a damp, cold, gray day and I took the ride in a sort of grim, long-suffering silence.

We walked past a shabby little brick house that no-body would want to buy, up a muddy path, through a stubby field to a ramshackle barn that looked as if it would collapse in the next high wind. When we reached the top of the hill from which Stanley had seen his "marvelous view," all we could see was fog.

My heart, which had been steadily sinking, dropped into my shoes. I tried not to let Stanley see how I felt, but I'm afraid I didn't succeed very well.

"Don't you think we should look further?" I asked faintly.

"Look further?" he cried. "This is exactly the place I've been looking for for years. Of course you can't see the view today, but across there is the Hudson, and Bear Mountain, and from the top of that hill where we're going to build our house you can see Anthony's Nose. Down there on the left is where we'll have a tennis court; those trees on the right are fruit trees—apples, pears, peaches and grapevines too. And down below are the most wonderful woods where we'll clear trails and we can all hike."

How glad I have been—many many times—that I let Stanley persuade me. That was thirty-seven years ago, and the place in Croton has not only long since repaid our original investment; it has done something more important. It has been a haven to which we went happily over the years, and to which I still go to find rest and peace and comfort in happy memories.

Disproving my gloomy prediction, Stanley sold the

brick house and a share in the land to Irving Schwarz-kopf, a civil engineer who became a devoted friend and an invaluable aid in solving many of the problems that beset a property owner. A small cabin was built in the woods within a few months, so that we could spend weekends there while the main house was being built. Stanley and the architect put their heads together to make that house the most comfortable and attractive refuge for our family and friends. Almost immediately it settled down in the surrounding shrubbery and lawn and looked as if it had always been there.

And I, in spite of my pessimism on that foggy day when I first looked at the place, came rapidly to share Stanley's enthusiasm. But he always teased me and never let me forget what a wet blanket I had been at first. Often when I would rhapsodize over a sunset, or the view, or the joy of a simple life in the country, he would smile and say, "Don't you think we should have looked further?"

The tennis court was duly built. Stanley played an unconventional, heady game; mine was more unconventional and less heady, but both Stanley and I could run, and neither of us let a ball get by without a struggle. We won a number of cups in lesser club-and-resort tournaments. We loved it and took on all comers until Stanley's heart attack in 1944.

The heart attack put a stop to playing tennis but not to clearing the woods and trails of fallen timber, sawing and bringing in logs for the fireplace, carrying up pails of water from the spring (he claimed it tasted so much better than water from a faucet), pruning fruit trees and helping our neighbors with any job that required his help.

Casey and I wrote a song "immortalizing" his activities, to one of his favorite tunes in *The Gondoliers*. It was sung at one of the many dinners given in Stanley's honor:

Up in Croton there's a haven
Where I like to loaf and rest.
Unobserved, I go unshaven
Shed my tie, my coat and vest.
Then, with hammer, saw and ax,
I'm all ready to relax.

While a weary world is yawning,
I get up at six each morning,
Don my khaki pants, a flannel shirt and boots.
In a hat attractive solely
'Cause the years have made it holey,
I engage in my relaxative pursuits.
First I probably will wander on the trail,
Maybe stirring up some partridges and quail;
Then I'll clear the fallen branches from the path,
The debris of a tempest's aftermath,
And I'll saw the solid timber
For it helps to keep me limber,
It's a very restful pastime and diminishes my weight,
Then some hefty logs I carry,
For it's beneficiary
For a guy who's on vacation and who wants to vegetate.

While with Nature I'm communing
I can always do some pruning,

The apple trees and grapevines need my care.
Then I go and see the neighbors
To assist them with their labors,
For there's often heavy damage to repair.
Then I carry pails of water from the spring
While the tunes of Gilbert-Sullivan I sing;
Though I'm often told my caroling is quaint,
And the songs I sing sound more like what they ain't.

Oh the city folks may talk
Of the beauties of New York,
But the pleasures of a weekend in the country are the best.
And the culminating pleasure that I treasure beyond measure
Is the gratifying feeling that I've had a perfect rest!

For ten years we spent our summers, as well as week-ends, in Croton and had hordes of visiting friends too much of the time. Myron would arrive from college with his gang, Casey with hers—neither of them having checked with us or each other as to who might be there. Up to a point we enjoyed it, but after a decade of running a cross between a roadhouse and a country club we got tired.

"Let's rent it," I suggested, "and move into the apartment over the garage where we shan't have room for guests." That was the first restful summer we had in Croton.

The next year Marian Ascoli, who rented the house, needed the apartment over the garage for servants, so we moved into the cabin in the woods. Our toilet was an outhouse, our bath a portable outdoor shower, our cooking was done over a kerosene stove or a hollow rock, and when we needed heat we got it from a kerosene heater. On a bitter cold night following a New Year's Eve party with friends at Croton we decided to spend the weekend in the cabin. We lit the heater, and Stanley filled a hot-water bottle for me, spilling a little of the water. In the morning my shoes were frozen to the floor. I looked at Stanley and he looked at me, and we both burst out laughing. The kerosene heater, which had burned all night, had smoked—and everything in the room, including us, was covered with soot. The following week Stanley ordered electricity installed.

Over the next few years we added two rooms to the cabin, and an honest-to-goodness bathroom, but we had sense enough not to let it turn into a weekend resort.

4

IS GOOD TO FORGET

Joji had been with us only a few months when we discovered that he was an artist and had considerable talent. We had already learned that this moon-faced little man could cook, serve, drive a car and perform all the odd jobs for which a houseman is called on, but we hadn't the slightest idea that he could paint.

One Saturday afternoon when Stanley and I came

home from the movies, we went into the kitchen for a snack and found Joji sitting in front of an improvised easel, painting a portrait in water colors. Next to him, on a table, stood a photograph of a Japanese boy which he was copying.

"Hokay, I paint in kitchen?" he asked. "Light more better here as my room."

"Of course it's okay," said Stanley. "I didn't know you were an artist."

"They send me night school for learning English. I like painting lessons more better." Deft, quick strokes of his brush brought out ivory-flesh tints, coppery-red hair. "You never see Japanese boy with red hair?" he asked.

"No. Who is it?"

"My boy," he said. "I got wife. No see for twenty-two years." His hand must have shaken, and a brush mark spoiled the mouth at which he was working. He groaned, took the picture from the easel and tore it up.

"Oh, Joji, that was so nice! Couldn't you have fixed it?" I asked.

"Can't fix water color. Anyway, no good, I try thousand times. Never right."

"Is the boy living with his mother?" I asked.

"Boy not living," he said shortly. "Now I fix dinner."

Our curiosity was piqued, so at dinner that night we questioned him. He had little to say of his early years, but we gathered they hadn't been easy. It wasn't until he was twenty-five that he got his first job in the United States with a well-to-do childless couple in Connecticut named Peterson. There was also a Swedish maid in the house, Helga Janssen—young, pretty, with red hair. She and Joji became interested in each other, they were married soon, and Stevie, the little Swedish-Japanese redhead, was eventually born.

"Beautiful boy, good, smart. When he's two he's smart like he was three, four," said Joji.

Quite naturally he became the pet of the household. Guests were always brought into the nursery to see the latest addition to the family, and Joji would burst with pride when "big shots" admired Stevie. "Is my boy!" he would boast.

One December morning when Stevie was about two and a half, he woke up cranky and wouldn't eat his breakfast. He was screaming when Helga picked him up and carried him into the nursery. " 'You bad boy,' she say and spank him. I get very mad. I grab her and slap her face. 'Stevie not bad,' I say. 'Maybe he have stomach ache.' "

That afternoon, while Joji drove Mrs. Peterson to the dentist, Helga took Stevie out for his usual walk. It was bitter cold, but Helga believed in fresh air for children. She stopped at a five-and-ten to do some shopping and brought Stevie home later than usual. Joji was in the hall waiting when they got back—Stevie was crying and coughing. Joji could see that he was sick and called a doctor.

It was pneumonia, and those were the prepenicillin days. They did everything the doctor told them to do, but Stevie grew worse. The next night, while the doctor was there, the boy died. Joji refused to believe it when the doctor told him his son was dead, and after the doctor left, Joji got into Stevie's bed with him.

"All night I hold Stevie. Try to make him warm. No good. Next morning I see is all over."

Desperately in need of comfort, he found none in Helga.

"She cry sometime, next minute she laugh, sing, joke with delivery boys. Why she don't suffer like me?"

Joji started drinking to escape his misery. He and Helga fought constantly. One morning he saw her go into Stevie's room with her mop and dustcloth. Joji followed her to the door and stood there, very drunk. She sang a gay little Swedish song as she dusted Stevie's chair, his table, his toys.

"Stop singing that damn song!" he ordered, but she kept right on. Joji lurched into the room, tore off her apron and stuffed it into her mouth.

"Now sing!" he shouted. "You kill my Stevie! You sing in this room once more, I kill *you*."

That afternoon she packed her things and left, never to be seen or heard of again. Soon after, Joji left the Petersons and took a job as a waiter for a time; then, until he came to us, he worked for another couple in Connecticut.

"Sometimes I think I not fair to Helga. She don't mean to kill Stevie. She don't know better. Maybe she feel bad like me." He sighed. "Helga is beautiful woman."

"Have you a picture of her?" I asked.

"I tear up. Throw away. No use keeping. Swede no good for Japanese. Japanese no good for Swede."

Joji's only tie with the past was the photograph of Stevie, which he placed on his bedside table so he could see it first thing in the morning and last thing at night. But it wasn't good enough. It didn't show the exciting red hair that, with the Japanese features, had distinguished Stevie from other children. If only he could have it in color!

One morning several months after he had told us the story he called me into the kitchen, where he was entertaining one of his Japanese friends.

"Madame, is my friend Naka. Naka is artist thousand time more better as me. Naka promise to make oil painting from my Stevie. He charge only for canvas." Joji beamed.

The two celebrated the pact over a succession of drinks. It was to be a large picture, and it grew as the evening wore on. It was to be life-size by the time Naka staggered out, the photograph carefully wrapped and stowed in a suitcase for safety.

During the weeks that followed, Joji could hardly restrain his impatience.

"Picture is good, I give Naka fifty dollars."

The next week: "I think I give Naka hundred dollars."

Some days later: "Is hokay I hang picture in kitchen, madame? I buy best frame. Gold."

"Of course it's okay," I said.

"Mr. Isaacs don't mind?"

"No, why should he?"

After a month of waiting: "Must be big picture. Is long time." Another week and no sign of the portrait. "I don't understand why picture take so long. You write Naka letter for me, madame?" I wrote a letter, and within a few days the answer came:

Joji:

Please excuse I don't write. Very drunk when I leave your house. I go Nagaki place, drink some more. Next day I look—I look every place for picture, for suitcase. Is no place. I know you like picture whole lots. Sorry, old man. Please excuse.

Naka

Joji's face twitched as he read. Then he laughed—Joji laughs when he's unhappy—it wasn't a pleasant laugh.

"Sorry, madame," he said and went to his room.

There followed a drinking bout that lasted several days. One morning at breakfast, after Joji had sobered up, he confided to us. "For me is like my red-haired Stevie never live. Before he only die. Now *is* no more. Naka kill him." He gave a profound sigh.

It seemed to us that he was overplaying the heavy-tragedy act; and Stanley said later, "Twenty years is a long time for deep mourning."

For several days Joji was morose and moody. But gradually the gloom lifted.

"You want I tell you something?" he asked one evening as he was serving dinner. And without waiting for the answer: "Maybe is good what Naka do. I'm much more happier now. Before is like I have a big stone inside. Every time I see my Stevie picture I think about bad time. Now is much more better. Almost"—he set the tray on the table—"almost—no, maybe I shouldn't say. But is true."

"What's true?" I prompted.

"Almost"—he shook his head sadly—"almost—I *forget* my red-hair Stevie! Is this bad? Is good? I think maybe is good."

"Yes," said Stanley, "it's good."

Joji smiled happily. He had Stanley's approval.

5

I PUT–I TAKE

Joji's weakness for liquor had often been troublesome for us. There was the time, for instance, when he went on an errand at six P.M. and hadn't returned by midnight. I called all the bars in the neighborhood, the emergency wards of two hospitals, then the police, but his trail had been lost. He staggered in about two and told me his story in the morning.

At one of the bars he had met a friend who took him to a meeting of Alcoholics Anonymous. There Joji had made a magnificent confession, recounting with more eloquence than veracity the story of his sordid life, how he had been a miserable drunkard and how he had been miraculously saved by A. A.

"I make fine speech," he told me. "Everybody clap."

Then he and his friend had gone to the nearest bar, where they celebrated Joji's oratory with further libations.

There had been other times like this—episodes which might be called the "little binges," without any serious repercussions. The two times that I remember with shudders were somewhat different.

When our daughter, Casey, became engaged to Snowden Herrick, I was naturally eager to meet Snow's mother, Elinore Herrick, the well-known labor arbiter, writer, lecturer, and a most impressive person. So one Friday night we invited Snow and her to dinner, which was a mistake. Friday is the day after Thursday, and Thursday was Joji's day off. Too often in those days I would get a familiar phone call Friday morning.

"Madame"—and Joji's voice would be thick—"I'm drunk again. You need me today?"

Usually I didn't, and told him to sleep it off. If I expected guests, and if he could navigate, he'd come home and somehow muddle through. If he couldn't, he'd say, "Sorry, madame, too impossible. I send friend." He had many friends and they had all cooked and served meals for us with varying success.

As Joji was about to leave the house on the Thursday before the eventful Friday, I told him about the dinner and stressed the necessity for sobriety.

"Hokay," he said blithely as he left, "I be good boy."

Friday morning dawned with no Joji to bring us breakfast and the newspapers. When he hadn't put in an appearance by ten o'clock I called Nagaki's, the combination club, bar and rooming house where most of the Japanese in this area used to spend their days off.

"May I speak to Joji?" I asked.

"Joji don't feel so good today," said Nagaki.

"Can't you sober him up?"

"I try. He maybe call later."

This sounded as though I would not be able to count on Joji, so I called all the cooks on my emergency list. None was free. I phoned Casey at her office and asked whether we hadn't better call the dinner off, or if not, eat at a restaurant. Her answer was no to both questions.

"I hate restaurants," she said, "and our house is so nice. I want Elinore to meet you and Daddy there. It's terribly important. I hardly know her, and somehow a public restaurant doesn't seem right."

"But how about the dinner? I'm a terrible cook, you know."

"Oh, you're not all *that* bad," Casey said. "I'll come over early and help with the cooking, and Snow and I'll do the dishes."

"All right, dear," I agreed meekly.

At eleven the phone rang. The voice was unmistakably Joji's.

"Yes, I know," I said before he had a chance to say anything. "You're drunk again. But you *must* come home. Don't you remember, the Herricks are coming tonight—Miss Casey's fiancé and his mother. You've *got* to make it!"

"Hokay. I come."

Half an hour later he reeled in, in no condition to work. I sent him to his room to sleep it off. Then I set the table, prepared the salad, celery, radishes. That much I can cook. At about three o'clock Joji had apparently made a miraculous recovery, and he shooed me out of the kitchen.

"Joji is fine," I said to Casey when she came in. "All you have to do is fix the flowers."

At seven-thirty the guests arrived.

Joji, impeccably dressed in his white coat and black tie, served the cocktails with his most delectable canapés. We chatted impersonally until dinner was announced. Then we took our places at the table and tried to make conversation. But even small talk seemed impossible without food in front of us.

Suddenly Joji appeared with the first course and announced in stentorian tones: "Everything under control!"

Joji rarely drank our liquor without permission, but cocktails left in a shaker he considered his property. Did he mix too much that night, or did we drink less than usual? At any rate, there was too much left—too much on top of what he'd already had. By the time he served the second course it had really taken effect. Instead of bringing the meat and vegetables on a platter, he reverted to a habit he had acquired years before in a small-town restaurant. Steak, potatoes and asparagus were arranged on plates, the five of them strung along his arm. He came weaving into the dining room, stopped at my side, and was about to unload my dish when he realized that he hadn't taken away the soup plates.

"That's all right, Joji," I said. "I'll collect them."

"No," he said very positively. "I put. I take." I knew by the tone of his voice that if I tried to do more it would make an awkward scene, so I sat in quiet trepidation while he proceeded.

He must have been a juggler once. Fascinated, we watched as he picked up a plate here, deposited one there, swinging, swaying. And with each operation he announced, "I put. I take."

Stanley did his best to divert Elinore's attention from the painful proceedings. He engaged Snow and her in a serious discussion—about politics, I think. I looked from one speaker to the other, but my mind was elsewhere. Through their conversation ran the refrain, "I put, I take. I take, I put." Joji kept saying it even when he wasn't doing it. He seemed to like the sound. Under other circumstances we would have enjoyed these antics and probably laughed. But now the atmosphere was tense.

We got through the salad course without incident. Then came a long wait, with much clattering of dishes offstage. As I was removing the salad plates to avoid future complications, there came a burst of song from the kitchen. Joji knew only one tune, and he sang it when he was especially pleased with himself.

I rang the bell for the fourth time. "Hokay," he shouted, "hokay," and made a triumphant entrance into the dining room.

The dessert, a semifrozen chocolate pudding surrounded by an intricate design of whipped cream, was in the center of a large platter balanced on his left forearm. On his right hand was a precariously stacked column of alternating plates and dessert bowls, five of each. He came to the table, his arms extended, waving them up and down.

"Pretty good, hey?"

"Quite remarkable," Stanley said frigidly.

"You know, boss, I'm drunk."

Stanley tried heavy sarcasm. "Are you really, Joji? No one would suspect it." Then, affecting a lighthearted gaiety I am sure he didn't feel, he added, "Well, how are we going to manage this?"

"Is easy. You take plate. I turn around. You take pudding."

We followed orders, but it took delicate maneuvering to preserve the necessary balance.

Elinore was next. With more force than was necessary she sliced off a portion, apparently loosening the mass from its moorings. At that moment a door slammed. Joji gave a start. The pudding shivered, shook, and then, as we all watched, petrified, it dramatically plunged into Elinore's capacious lap.

There was a moment of shocked silence. Then, "Oh, Joji," Stanley groaned, in despair.

"Hold everything," Joji commanded, sliding the plates and saucers onto the table. Then, spooning the pudding from Elinore's lap to the platter, he announced with each motion, "I put, I take; I take, I put."

The second grand debacle came in '56, when a dinner for some of our most special friends was a complete flop. Stanley and I stood facing each other as the door closed on the last guest.

"What on earth happened?" he asked.

"It wasn't Joji's fault, really. Those stupid waitresses brought down half-empty cocktail glasses and gave them to him."

"He didn't have to drink them. He knows what liquor does to him. Joji's never before made such a mess of a meal—even when he was plastered."

"He didn't cook this one. He passed out cold. The waitresses took over and they didn't know much about cooking."

"You don't have to tell me that. Nothing was fit to eat. It was an absolute disgrace. And for that very special party!"

"What do you want me to do?"

"What do you think?"

"I suppose you want me to fire him."

"Don't you think you should?"

"No, I don't." I thought of my weeks in the hospital, when Joji came every day with some delicacy he had prepared, to tempt my finicky appetite; of the summers in Croton, where he grew bigger, better and sweeter fruits of the earth for our enjoyment; of his invaluable services throughout Stanley's many campaigns; of his loving care of our series of pets and of us. The word "no" was missing in his vocabulary. So he drank. To my way of thinking, his virtues far outweighed his one and only vice. He was a part of our life—most of the time making it easier for us, often lending spice to it, occasionally complicating it. "He's so wonderful when he's sober, which is most of the time," I said.

"And completely unreliable when he's drunk," said Stanley.

"I know. I feel just as awful about tonight as you do."

"You don't or you'd fire him. I can't take this sort of thing!"

"All right," I said, "I'll fire him."

In the morning I was thinking of asking Stanley to relieve me of my promise, and he would have, I'm sure. He got over his occasional fits of wrath very quickly. But then I had to cook breakfast, and what I saw downstairs was positively revolting. The waitresses hadn't bothered to look for dish towels and had used my monogrammed napkins to dry the dishes; the napkins were piled on the kitchen counter, still wet, and dirty; our three sets of china (kitchen, everyday and best) were all mixed up and shoved wherever the girls found room for them; and my flat silver was lumped together with the plated ware and the kitchen knives and forks. When I sorted them out, I found that four of the sterling pieces were missing. I searched high and low in vain. There was no other place to look but in the garbage. I thought I couldn't face it, and so I woke Joji up. He looked at me with glassy eyes, groaned and went back to sleep. Should I forget the silver? No, it couldn't be replaced. I put on rubber gloves and went to work, and found the missing pieces in the first and last can. But never again!

My scavenging hardened my heart, and when Joji came to my room after lunch, looking gray and miserable, I didn't flinch. "I've overlooked a lot of things, Joji," I said sternly, "but last night was too much!"

"You fire me?"

"Yes, Joji."

"You're right. I'm just a drinking bum."

"The night of Miss Casey's engagement party was bad enough. But this, when I told you how important—"

"Hokay! Hokay! I'm fired. When you want me to go?"

"There's no hurry."

"You like I stay till you get somebody?"

"I *would* like that."

"You want I call Nagaki? Always he have somebody out of job."

"Yes, I wish you would."

Joji looked pensive. "Maybe Nobu can come."

"That would be fine," I said, remembering a marvelous dinner Nobu had prepared one time when Joji wasn't functioning.

"Nobu is good cook, is honest, is clean, never drinks. He speak English lots more better as me. I call up now." Presently he returned. "Nobu come three o'clock." And he did. An hour later Joji knocked on my door. "I go now," he said.

"I hope you get a good job," and I handed him a reference and his check.

"I take little vacation—one week, two weeks. I gonna miss you whole lots, madame," he said.

"I'll miss you too, Joji."

"No, no, you don't miss me. Nobu is fine cook. Lots more better as me."

"I'll miss you anyway. You've been here a long, long, time." We looked at each other sadly.

"Well, goodbye," he said quickly, shook my hand and was gone.

A pall hung over dinner that night. Nobu's cooking was flawless but much too rich for our tastes. A five-course banquet—we didn't touch the dessert.

At about ten o'clock the next morning the phone rang.

"Is Joji, madame. How's Mr. Isaacs?"

Stanley M. Isaacs, 1922

BELOW: *A summer weekend in Bear Mountain Park—the inevitable hike.* RIGHT: *Stanley and Edith Isaacs in Croton, May 1930.* BOTTOM: *The house in Croton.*

AN FISHER

ABOVE: *Stanley in Croton.*
RIGHT: *The irrepressible Joji.*

TOP: *Stanley showing a group of visitors the East River Drive during its construction, April 1941.* ABOVE: *Mayor Fiorello La Guardia opening a section of the Drive with as much space as possible between Stanley and Robert Moses.*

Stanley in his office.

LIONEL DOTTIN

LIONEL DOTTIN

ABOVE: *Stanley with
Governor Nelson Rockefeller.*
RIGHT: *With Senator
Jacob Javits.*

TOP LEFT: *The Isaacs house
on 96th Street.* BOTTOM LEFT:
*Stanley M. Isaacs
Neighborhood Center.*

ILSA HOFMAN

ABOVE: *Mr. and Mrs. Stanley Isaacs on their fiftieth wedding anniversary, with their children, Casey Isaacs Herrick and Myron Isaacs.* LEFT: *Stanley with John V. Lindsay.*

"He's fine."

"How's Timmy?" Timmy was a dog Joji had given us.

"Timmy's fine."

"How's Nobu getting along?"

"He's a little fancy for us, but I guess he'll work out all right."

"I miss you all so lots, madame."

"We miss you, too, Joji."

There was a silence; then, "Well, goodbye," and Joji hung up.

I entered the kitchen diffidently, dreading the prospect of training a new man.

Nobu was looking over the supplies in one of the closets.

"Good morning," I said.

"You have an account at Gristedes?" was his answer.

"Yes," I said.

"I go marketing this morning," he announced.

"Shall we make out a list?" I asked.

"Not necessary. I know what I need."

I decided to trust him. After all, Joji had said he was honest. And he was, but not what you would call frugal. I found my shelves laden with rare and expensive delicacies.

Lunch for me alone consisted of grapefruit, a squab, fresh asparagus, and strawberries out of season.

Dinner that night: mushroom pâté, filet mignon, artichokes and baked Alaska.

The next morning I bearded Nobu in his den. "You're a wonderful cook, Nobu, but we'd rather have simpler meals."

"I see," he said, "something like beef stew?"

"Yes," I said, "that would be fine," not knowing that the stew would be made with mushrooms, truffles and cognac, would be preceded by turtle soup and followed by salad and chocolate soufflé.

When I protested, Nobu said, "I give you everything just like Joji tell me."

Foxy Joji. I had begun to suspect a plot, but I thought I'd let it run its course until Stanley revolted.

I didn't have to wait long.

The next night Nobu served oysters for his first course. "Oysters!" Stanley said angrily, getting up from the table. "Didn't you tell him we never have shellfish in this house?"

"I did. But Nobu never pays any attention to my instructions."

"Well, let's go to a restaurant and get a good plain steak. And get that crazy man out of the house as fast as you can."

"Okay," I said.

"Do you think Joji has taken another job?" Stanley asked.

"I don't think so," I said.

"You'd like him back, wouldn't you?"

"I certainly would. Wouldn't you?"

"I suppose," he said, smiling.

I hugged him.

The following morning there was the usual phone call. "Would you like to come back, Joji?" I asked. I heard a click as he hung up the receiver, and in two minutes flat he was at the door. He had been calling from a bar around the corner.

"Joji," I asked, "how could you recommend that man to me. Nobu's absolutely impossible."

"I only tell you truth, madame, I say is honest, clean, is good cook, don't drink."

"Did you tell him what to cook for us?"

"Maybe, a little. Anyway, I know he don't last too long. Nobu never keeps job more as one, two weeks."

WHOLLY MOSES

Robert Moses, who wielded the greatest power of any single man under a succession of mayors and governors, holding multiple jobs and titles, was a lavish spender of the city's funds. Stanley did his best to curb him, and became something of a thorn in his side—and vice versa.

When Moses presented his plans for the development of the Belt Parkway to the Board of Estimate in 1938, there was general approval, but Stanley questioned the staggering cost. However, he voted for it. The following year Moses came back to the board, asking for many millions more to finish the job. "But you told us last year that the money you asked for then would do the whole job," said Stanley. Moses laughed. "If I had told you the total cost, you would never have voted for it. Now you've got to let me finish it."

Moses was infuriated when Stanley opposed his plan for a Battery-Brooklyn Bridge, in 1939. In a letter to LaGuardia, Stanley argued that the approaches to the bridge would seriously injure a large number of important office buildings, costing the owners many millions, which would be reflected in heavy reduction of taxable values. Stanley pointed out that the bridge approach would blight that section and would use land as valuable as any in Manhattan, whereas a tunnel would occupy no public lands for any purpose except an underground easement.

Also, Moses' bill provided that the city would pay all excess if the cost of the land acquired north of Battery Park should exceed the estimate, and Stanley reminded LaGuardia that Moses' estimate of the Belt Parkway had been only a fraction of the actual cost. The simple and natural solution, Stanley thought, was for the Triborough Bridge Authority, independently financed, to pay all costs.

Moses' anger increased when the U.S. Government, for military reasons, upheld Stanley's view that the approaches to a bridge would be ruinous. They approved the substitute plan for a tunnel, which was, in fact, constructed.

During the construction of the East River Drive, Stanley okayed almost all the parks and playgrounds that Moses asked for along the drive, with a few notable exceptions. One was a park that Moses suggested be placed just above the Fulton Fish Market, where Stanley claimed there were too few residents to make a playground worthwhile. The battle became loud and vituperative, and they finally decided to leave the decision to LaGuardia.

One morning Stanley, Moses and the Mayor drove down to the area in question, Moses peering out of the car anxiously for a sight of some poor little waif playing marbles in the gutter, or at least a baby carriage parked outside a pool parlor. Not a sign of residential life—just lines and lines of trucks and carts plying their wholesale trade with the fish market.

LaGuardia didn't waste any time. "You lose, Bob," he said.

In another episode, Moses accused Stanley in a letter of being anti-playgrounds, because, he claimed, he was destroying them and offering no substitute; Moses said Stanley should stop further construction of the East River Drive rather than proceed at the expense of local recreation.

Stanley obtained the exact figures from Commissioner Walter Binger and answered Moses:

We have eliminated the very small playground which you operated just north of Carl Schurz Park between 89th and 90th Streets . . . This playground covered 0.38 of an acre. The plans for the Drive, however, increased the area of Carl Schurz Park at this point by 1.86 acres. Part of this increased area you are using as a playground for older boys and girls and adults.

The plans for the area between 90th and 99th Streets involve the elimination of three small areas, the aggregate of which is 0.75 of an acre. We are providing two new parks between 95th and 97th Streets with an area of 2.65 acres . . .

In connection with the Harlem River Drive, our present plans involve the destruction of 2.14 acres of playground space, and the development of approximately 21.75 acres of new playground space. This is ten for one.

All of this makes perfectly nonsensical most of the statements in your letter and the perfectly silly accusations that they involve.

In response to a request from Moses' office later that year Stanley wrote a courteous letter acquiescing in all but one of Moses' requisitions. Stanley granted: a park area between 49th and 51st Streets, a promenade between 23rd and 25th Streets, parks from 49th to 51st Streets, parks from 54th to 58th Streets. Just the area from 30th to 34th Streets, which Moses had requested for a park, Stanley decided was unsuitable, as that section was to be developed for commercial purposes.

"I want you to know," wrote Stanley, "that in meeting your views all along the East River Drive, I am, of course, adding quite substantially to its cost . . . The parks are worth it, but on the other hand, the cost of the drive goes up just that much. Accordingly, I will want your help if I need more money for the drive as a result of areas taken for parks. I take for granted that I will have your co-operation . . ."

That was taking too much for granted. Moses' answer was another bombshell. Among other things, he wrote that he saw no justification for building a speedway along the East River, pre-empting most of the water-front for automobiles and leaving some of it for industry, without providing anything for local recreation. He went on to say that he thought Stanley was ducking responsibility for paying the cost of incidental walks, play areas and landscaping, and ended up by stating that he had always understood Stanley claimed to be a friend of the little fellow, but he was beginning to have some doubts about it. This letter I found among Stanley's papers filed under N (*Nonsense—more Moses*).

In the midst of all these quarrels are two cheerful notes. One was from Bob to Stanley, accompanying a Christmas plant, which Moses sent on behalf of his department. The note expressed gratitude for "the helpful and pleasant relationship" of the two departments throughout the year. And from Stanley to Bob:

Dec. 21, 1939

Thanks so much for the lovely plant that you sent me for Christmas and for all that you say. I, too, have enjoyed working with you and look forward to a very pleasant continuance of our relationship during the coming year.

The flowers on the Christmas plant had hardly had time to fade when there was another explosion in Stanley's office. Moses had written a letter saying he didn't like Stanley's plans for the East River Drive at 91st Street at all—that it was quite apparent a mess was going to be created which would seriously affect the Triborough Bridge, etc., etc., etc.

One of the compromises made at the expense of the ordinary citizen was the rise in subway fares, and Stanley was infuriated. In a letter to Irving Baldinger he wrote:

Moses' program calls for an increased fare by the subway rider to relieve the City's debt limit from the $25,000,000 subway investment, so that the City can borrow more money which will be invested in highways, bridges, parkways, etc., for the motorist, for which the motorist will not be asked to contribute a nickel. Why the motorist should be given a free ride and the straphanger asked to pay the full capital cost of the subway investment certainly cannot be explained decently. The subways are services which the City renders to all of its people and which the City can well afford to subsidize. They are a great integrating force that unites all boroughs, and the maintenance of the current rate of fare can, from my point of view, be fully justified by this broad advantage.

The Battle of Van Cortlandt was another one that Stanley lost. He urged Newbold Morris, a member of the Planning Commission, to delay action on Moses' plan, which was being rushed through without even a hearing. If Moses' plan went through, the Major Deegan Expressway would bisect Van Cortlandt Park, damaging its wild beauty and ruining it as a playground for children.

"I frankly feel outraged by what is being done," said Stanley, but Moses' iron whim ruled the commission. Stanley got his hearing, and Moses got his way—his Express Way.

✍ Then there was the famous Battle of Central Park, another chapter in Isaacs vs. Moses. There were few enough children's playgrounds in the park—no other so accessible for the mothers and children of the West Sixties as the one adjacent to the Tavern-on-the-Green.

One summer day in 1956 our friend Eleanor Sanger, whose apartment overlooked the Tavern, called Stanley to say that Moses wanted to convert this playground into a parking lot for the Tavern. She said a group of mothers had banded together to ask Stanley to take preventive steps. Another call came early the next morning from an outraged Eleanor: "A bulldozer has just arrived in the playground and is starting to uproot the trees."

Stanley told her to round up her group of mothers and rush them over to the playground, with their babies in their carriages. Stanley got there in record time—to find the bulldozer driver furious but impotent. "What can I do? I can't run over all them babies."

Stanley followed up the resulting newspaper uproar with a letter to the Mayor:

Hon. Robert F. Wagner

Dear Mr. Mayor:

I wish to protest with all the vehemence at my command the wanton destruction of park property which your Park Commissioner is about to commit. To provide additional parking space for the Tavern-on-the-Green, he is about to destroy time-honored trees, uproot bushes and dig up the land nearby. He is ready to deprive the City, and especially those who make extensive use of this part of the Park, of a substantial area, to provide more room for the patrons of a favored restaurant.

Park property should not be used for this purpose, certainly not Central Park. Central Park is the sacred heritage of our generation. No one—not even the Lord High Park Commissioner—should be permitted to destroy its beauties for such an unworthy purpose.

I am told that you suggested to those who have already protested to you, that they should discuss the matter with the Park Commissioner. They asked a hearing, and his immediate answer was to put a bulldozer on the job. I ask you, who alone have the power to do so, to stop this at once . . . The people who do not want to see this act of vandalism performed should at least be granted a hearing. Overnight the Commissioner is about to commit greater damage than all the youthful vandals (of whom he constantly and properly complains) perform in a year.

Faithfully yours,

Stanley M. Isaacs

A board was appointed to study the situation—and their verdict to preserve the playground didn't do much to sweeten Bob Moses' disposition.

There were a number of other more or less minor controversies between Moses and Stanley. One I remember well: whether to use the rubble from the bombed city of Bristol, England, as fill for the East River Drive —Stanley for; Moses against. It was indeed used. And when the plaque memorializing the event was dedicated, Moses was conspicuous by his absence. Gracie Fields sang, the Mayors of New York and Bristol spoke. It was one of the most moving of the openings I attended.

On the whole, their battle score was pretty much tied. On the matter of retaining the Battery aquarium, Stanley lost. This was evened out by his victory on the question of how to use the space adjacent to Bellevue Hospital, which had been cleared during the construction of the East River Drive. It could be used either for a public park or for the hospital staff and patients. Stanley and the hospital won. He also won his fight for "Shakespeare in the Park."

In 1956, when Joseph Papp conceived the idea of "Shakespeare in the Park," he came to Stanley for help in putting it over. This Stanley gave enthusiastically, finding soon that Moses led the opposition. But Papp won out and Mr. Shakespeare has been flourishing in ever-expanding performances on ever-expanding stages.

There *were* occasions when Stanley and Moses agreed. The entrances and exits of the transverse road through Central Park at 96th Street had been planned in the thirties, in the horse-and-buggy days, and were a source of aggravation to drivers, who were frequently held up by long lines of cars and trucks unable to move in either direction.

This was an obvious nuisance, which Stanley determined to eliminate. He laid his plans for the widening and relocation of the exits and entrances before the Mayor, stating that Moses approved the program and was co-operating fully. The Mayor and the Board of Estimate approved, and the project was accomplished with the help of W.P.A. workers at low cost to the city. It became a model for similar changes in the entrances and exits of the three other transverse roads through the park.

Moses was famous for an unbridled tongue. Anyone who disagreed with him was a crook, a villain, a nitwit or whatever damning epithet came to his mind. His small daughter, with Moses on a motor trip on one occasion, was quoted as saying "Daddy, why is everyone who passes us either a louse or a son of a bitch?"

But as the years went by, the Isaacs/Moses feud seemed to abate. Stanley admired Moses, and their social relationship was friendly. As a matter of fact, our son-in-law, Snowden Herrick, had worked for Moses before the war—long before Casey met him—and they had always kept up their friendship. This gave rise to a rather uncomfortable weekend, just after one of Stanley and Moses' most publicized and bitter battles, when

Moses was staying with Elinore Herrick at the same time that Casey and her family were there. She called Stanley up that evening and said, "Daddy, that S. O. B. is so nice—he spent an hour last night reading bedtime stories to Mike. I wish I didn't have to dislike him."

Scattered in among their voluminous peppery correspondence, I found quite a number of very friendly letters, with promises to co-operate in every possible way.

In answer to Stanley's letter on his seventieth birthday, Moses wrote the following:

Dear Stanley,

It was most kind and friendly of you to take the time at a busy season to write to an old friend. I appreciate it no end, echo your sentiments and repudiate any suggestion of future disagreements, and surely those in the past were trivial, minor and in any event quite forgotten.

Bob

While the differences were far from trivial, Stanley welcomed Moses' friendly overtures, since he had a healthy respect for the man's ability, but he reserved tacitly the right to future battles. Slum clearance under Title I was one of the biggest issues of the fifties. Stanley spoke out incessantly against the ruthless displacement of people. To him the bulldozers seemed busier with the removal of people than with the bricks and mortar, or at least as busy. He was shocked that in the wake of slum clearance, people were left without a place to go, that often thousands disappeared in the shuffle without leaving a forwarding address. He deplored the fact that his great city of New York was at the time the only large city without a relocation bureau, and spearheaded the fight to get one.

Stanley wanted slower demolition to allow time to find homes for displaced tenants. It was his original idea to retain many of the salvageable houses in a given area and at the same time allow tenants to remain in their homes while planned renovation took place. People always came first with him. Not with Moses. The whole area had to be cleared, and at once.

But when Moses was under fire for alleged mishandling of the Title I program, Stanley stood firmly behind him. "Bob Moses is an extremely capable man," he said. "Properly controlled, he is a great asset to the city."

Moses proved himself an asset many times, and whenever he did, Stanley was there to support him. It was Moses' idea, for example, to acquire the Jamaica race track for city housing, and Stanley was delighted. Since it was a huge area, it could provide extensive housing for tenants without dislocating a single person. Stanley went all out to back him, and today a huge middle-income integrated development is a reality there, with 25 percent occupancy by minority groups.

7

EASY GO

From April through June, Joji always had a one-track mind: a race-track mind. Although he swore off the ponies a dozen times a year, he was always on hand for the first and last races of the season.

The names of horses intrigued him. He always bet on the names of his friends, with varying success. One season there was a Busy Stan in the field, and whenever he was slated to run, Joji would come to our door and ask, "You *busy* today, Mr. Isaacs?"

He always was and would say so.

"Good, I bet on Busy Stan."

I don't know how often Stanley misled him, but Busy Stan never won a race for him.

"You not busy enough," Joji would say sadly.

And if I ever spoke of a dream I remembered he would interpet it as an omen. But I dropped the whole subject after mentioning at breakfast one morning that I had dreamed about a man who was wearing three hats.

"Three hats!" said Joji excitedly and promptly put money on Number 3 in every race and a whopping amount on Number 3 in the third race. They all lost.

"You don't dream very good, madame," he said, frankly showing his disappointment in me.

There were times when he won, of course. His bets with the local bookie were soberly planned in advance, but at the race track it was different. He would get excited and lose his head.

"I win the first race," he would tell me later. "I put all on second race. Win second race, put all on third. Many times I win until last race. Then lose everything." And he would laugh, as though it were the best joke in the world.

"But why, why don't you put half your winnings aside each time?"

"You know me, madame. I'm gambler."

Occasionally, of course, he would win the last race,

but too often he didn't. There was the time when he finished with over a thousand dollars, and at the end of the day a man at the clubhouse offered him a drink.

"Looks like nice feller," said Joji the next morning. "He buy me a drink. I buy him a drink. I wake up when taxi driver ask me where I'm going. I tell him and he bring me home. I have nothing in my pockets for paying fare. Thousand dollars gone. Driver say, 'Hokay, the feller who put you in taxi pay me five bucks to take home a drunk.' *I* wasn't drunk. You know me, madame. It take more as two shots to make *me* drunk. That sonabitch give me knockout drops for sure."

Joji's really sensational coup happened during the summer of 1946. Stanley and I always gave him a vacation when we took ours. The day before we were to leave, Joji came to my room.

"Hokay I start my vacation a day ahead?"

"Of course," I said.

"I go race track. New horse running—Lucky Stan."

"Any relation to Busy Stan?"

"Same owner."

"Well, don't count too much on the name. Remember, Busy Stan never did anything for you."

"How much money in Isaacs bank?" he asked.

Isaacs bank started in Joji's early days with us, when he did considerable drinking and gambling, and I persuaded him to leave a part of his salary with Stanley to be saved up for his "dream"—a trip to Japan. I phoned Stanley, who gave me the figure. "You've got a hundred and fifty-five dollars saved," I said.

"And you give me vacation money ahead of time, yes? That's two hundred and fifty-five."

"It's up to you, Joji. But how about Japan?"

"Next month I start saving."

"How many times have you started?"

"Hokay. Mr. Isaacs keep five dollars for Japan. Give me two hundred fifty."

I sighed and gave him a check.

I met Stanley at a cocktail party, and when we came home we found Joji standing in front of our house, talking to a man we had never seen before. Later we learned he was the bartender from around the corner. We saw the man stoop several times and pick up something from the sidewalk. Joji was very drunk, and he was pulling a wad of money out of a bulging pocket and then shoving it back. He pulled another wad out of another pocket and shoved that back, dropping bills on the sidewalk at each operation. There were tens, twenties, fifties. The man helped us pick them up and handed them to me. I put them into my bag.

"What happened, Joji?" I asked.

"Lucky Stan win," he shouted. "I'm rich man. Big shot!"

At that point the man started to go away. "Wait a minute," said Stanley. "I saw you putting some of that money in your pocket."

"I was just keeping it for Joji until he gets sober," the man replied, pulling out a fifty-dollar bill and giving it reluctantly to Stanley.

"I want all of it," Stanley persisted, "or I'll call that cop." I looked toward the corner. There was no policeman, but Stanley's bluff worked. The man took out a hundred ninety dollars more, gave it to Stanley and walked off, cursing us under his breath.

We piloted Joji into the kitchen, where he told me the story.

"I put all two hundred fifty dollars on Lucky Stan, on the nose. Long shot. Fourteen to one. He win. I'm rich man. Big shot!" He laughed delightedly.

"Two hundred and fifty dollars! Fourteen to one! That's—that's—" I tried to figure it out in my head but gave up. "That's thirty-five hundred dollars," said Stanley, "enough to pay for your trip to Japan!"

"Sure thing," said Joji, once more pulling bills out of his pocket, and dropping several.

"You give Mr. Isaacs three thousand dollars to keep for Japan, and you'll have five hundred left for your vacation."

"No, no, no, no! You never know what happen when you go away. Maybe I be sick."

"But thirty-five hundred dollars! You can't spend it all in two weeks."

"Never know," he said stubbornly and shoved the money back in his pocket. "Now I go Greenwich Village," he announced.

"Not the way you are, Joji," said Stanley. "You've got to get sobered up. You take a good rest before you go there."

"Hokay. I take little sleep."

I later regretted that we hadn't picked his pockets while he lay there unconscious. He never would have known the difference, and the money would have stayed safely in the Isaacs bank, but taking it while he was sleeping was too much like stealing. As it was, what with the money Stanley had got back from the bartender and what I had picked up from the kitchen floor, we had four hundred and ten dollars stashed away for him.

A few hours later he left for Greenwich Village, taking I don't know how much of his wealth. He said it was two or three hundred dollars, but it must have been more or he couldn't have done all he did. He told us about it later: a champagne dinner at Cinderella for ten or twelve of the habitués—on Joji. "All girls crazy about me," he said. "Make me stand on table. Sing 'He's a Good Jolly Feller,' about *me!*" It was touching how much this purchased praise meant to him.

An especially pretty girl named Francine managed to push the other girls out of the way and took Joji over as her special property. Before the evening ended, she and Joji had arranged to go to Saratoga the next day, and Joji came back to our house and got the rest of his money for the trip. They stayed at the best hotel, he told us when he came back.

"We have dozen fresh towels every day," he said. "We have breakfast in bed. We go races every day. Win, lose, win, lose. One week money is all gone. Francine gone too. I come home. Now I'm poor man again."

"You spent all that money, Joji?" asked Stanley.

"When I'm drunk, I don't know what I do," he said sadly.

I could see that he needed a bracer, and I told him about the four hundred and ten dollars of his money that we had. "And that," I said firmly, "we're going to keep for your trip to Japan."

"All?" he asked, aghast.

"Of course," said Stanley.

"All is too much! Trip can wait. Japan haven't see me for forty year. Can wait another year. How about you give me half, Mr. Isaacs?"

Stanley looked at me helplessly. "I guess you have to," I said.

He gave him two hundred and five dollars.

"Thanks whole lots," Joji said. "You my best friends."

An hour later he came breathlessly to our room. "Lucky Stan running again today! Is *my* horse. Hokay I take all four hundred dollars? I put on nose and win again."

"Oh, Joji," I groaned. "Won't you ever learn?"

"No, madame."

"Well, it's your money," said Stanley.

But it wasn't for long.

Joji never learned not to gamble and not to be dazzled by a pretty face, but I came to believe that he got his money's worth in those brief splurges when, for a little while, he was a big shot. And fortunately he had a sense of humor about it.

A few weeks later, on his day off, he came to my door wearing his best made-to-order suit, a nylon shirt and a Sulka tie.

"I look hokay?" he asked.

"Very nice," I said.

"Like big shot?"

"Definitely—like a very big shot."

"I take a taxi all the way to Jamaica."

"And you'll give the driver a dollar tip."

"Two dollars on way back if I win."

He did win again and told me about it the next day.

Again he went to his favorite nightspot, Cinderella, where by now the proprietor and regulars all knew him.

"The headwaiter introduce me to very pretty girl," he told me. " 'Joji,' he say, 'I want you to meet the nicest little girl that ever come here. Malvina,' he say, 'this is Joji, one of our best customers. I want you should be nice to him.'

" 'Pleased to meet you,' I say. 'You are very beautiful. Are you movie actress?'

" 'Oh no,' she say.

" 'Model?'

" 'No,' she say, 'I'm writer.'

" 'Writer,' I say. 'Big shot.'

" 'Not big shot,' she say, nice and modest, 'just writer. What you do?'

"If I tell truth, is my finish. 'I banker in Wall Street,' I say.

" 'My!' she say. 'Millionaire!'

"I remember how you always talk small. 'No million-aire. Only comfortable off,' I say.

" 'All bankers is millionaire,' she say.

" 'I never count,' I say, and she laugh. She laugh like a bell. I treat her champagne dinner. I love her very much. She like me. I think next time I see her I ask her she should marry me."

Joji's romances were never serious. Whenever he met an attractive girl he promptly fell in love with her, and as promptly fell out again. But Malvina had really made an impression, and Joji kept going back to the Cinderella in the hope of seeing her again. In vain.

But one day weeks later he came back from marketing in great excitement. "Who you think I see Gristedes' just now?" he asked.

"I can't imagine, Joji."

He paused dramatically before he announced, "Malvina! Girl I meet at Cinderella."

"Congratulations!"

"She no writer, no big shot. She waitress for Martins on Park Avenue."

"Well," I said, "you're no rich Wall Street banker, so that makes you even. Did you admit it?"

"Sure," he answered, grinning. "But I come out ahead —way ahead. Malvina ask what help my boss have. I tell her, 'We have cook, we have butler, we have houseman, we have gardener, we have chauffeur.' I don't tell her all of them is me. I make one mistake. I should tell her we have lady's maid. I zip you up the back sometimes."

8

DEMOTION

Stanley's first year in the Council was a terrific letdown from the Borough Presidency. The United States had entered the war, and Stanley chafed at having no part in it. He offered his services, writing to friends, acquaintances and strangers:

September 14, 1942

Colonel Edward S. Greenbaum

Dear Eddie:

. . . I am not at all satisfied with my work today. The New York City Council is a bore. I am a minority member of a powerless body, with only one or two people to work with for whom I have real respect.

Law practice, which I resumed, does not interest me. Naturally what I really want is the opportunity of being of direct service in this war. There is plenty to do here but I am stymied. I want to know if there is any real opportunity for me in the War Department, either as a commissioned officer or otherwise.

While I realize I have somewhat limited qualifications, my experience in the Borough President's office involved administrative work of substantial importance, with a large staff. I should not appraise my own record, but I know that the job I did was approved as sound and constructive by those qualified to judge. A great deal of work was planned and executed speedily, and much money saved. My office worked well with other City departments and Government agencies. General Somervelle, who handled WPA here, I am sure will confirm this.

During the last war, I was Chairman of Draft Board 164, and take pride in the fact that it was run efficiently with a volunteer staff and cost the government less than any other draft board in New York State. I resigned from the board in 1918 to serve as a volunteer in the office of the Secretary of War.

. . . I have known Secretary Stimson for many years, but casually, and Judge Patterson too; Mrs. Roosevelt, Samuel Rosenman, Anna Rosenberg and many others who are today of considerable importance in the war effort. How well they think of me, of course, I do not know.

I am in fine shape physically—played tennis (singles as well as doubles) all summer, climbed mountains, chopped down trees and cleared brush, and I think could pass any reasonable test.

I do not want to follow the usual routine, visit those I know in Washington, and end by being somewhat of a nuisance to a great many busy people. Accordingly, I am concentrating on you, to ask you if you think there is any opportunity for me in a job that I could do well, and that could consume full energy; and if so, how I can work it out without going through that process.

I have no substantial outside income, but could get along on a moderate salary.

In any event, I hope you will answer me—and with complete frankness—at your convenience . . .

> Sincerely,
> Stanley M. Isaacs

Colonel Greenbaum regretfully turned him down because of his age, but Stanley made several attempts to get into other branches of the war effort. The answer was always the same. Although he was unsuccessful in giving his services to his country, he did manage to give his drop of over-age blood.

October 6, 1942

Mr. Earle Boothe:

Dear Mr. Boothe:

I have been privileged to give my blood twice to the Red Cross—once on July 7th and once on September 9th. I attained my sixtieth birthday on September 27th and therefore under your rules would not be eligible to give a third donation early in November, which I want and hope to do. I am in first-class condition. I can assure you my blood supply is ample, and just as serviceable as it was a few weeks before my sixtieth birthday. Under the circumstances, I ask the privilege of calling again during the first two weeks of November.

Sincerely,

Stanley M. Isaacs

Happily, permission was granted. That was the extent of war service that he was allowed to give, but Stanley was not one to rail against fate. He accepted the inevitable and made the most of his opportunities in the Council. His reputation and influence increased steadily throughout his twenty years there. First a member of the minority, then the minority leader, frequently the only Republican in the Council, he served on every committee, only once missing a committee or Council meeting—and that was because of illness.

Actually, the City Council job became, in a way, almost as satisfying as the Borough Presidency. The newspapers were intrigued with the situation of the lone Republican in a den of Democrats, and they covered his activities in the greatest detail. They enjoyed Stanley's sense of humor and played him up when he poked fun at the Establishment. When the Council, in accordance with the wishes of the Mayor, changed the name of Sixth Avenue to Avenue of the Americas, Stanley promptly and solemnly introduced a measure to change the name of the Avenue of the Americas to Sixth Avenue. The newspapers had a field day.

Among the minority leader's prerogatives was the appointment of a messenger, whose duty it was to run errands for the minority leader. Michigan Brown was the superannuated messenger of a succession of minority leaders, and though Stanley had no use for his services he hadn't the heart to discharge him. When, in 1952, he was retired, the news went out to Republican and Liberal district leaders, who besieged Stanley with applicants for the job. This was Stanley's answer to one of them:

December 4, 1952

Mr. Murray Baron
Dear Murray:
I have been giving really conscientious thought to the problem of filling that "messenger" vacancy in my

office of Minority Leader of the City Council. I can't tell you how much it has troubled me . . .

I just cannot waste the City's money nor spend it in a way that I think extravagant. When I was Borough President, I eliminated several exempt jobs. After a few months' experience I found one of my appointees really useless to me and in due course removed him, even though he was the husband of a good Republican District Leader, who never forgave me. A still greater offense was my conclusion that I did not need to fill the vacancy it created.

This Administration is headed for the rocks financially. One obvious reason is the number of unnecessary jobs which it maintains to take care of political friends. I can't attack it for waste and at the same time fill a post I honestly do not feel that I need to fill. You and others in the Liberal Party will, I am afraid, feel that I am doing you an injustice and think me quixotic. Nevertheless, I cannot reconcile myself to any other course.

I like the three candidates that you sent me, especially the last one—but nevertheless I can hardly change my attitude because I approve the individual who has applied for the post. I am *really* sorry if I disappoint you.

Sincerely yours,

Stanley M. Isaacs

Stanley repeatedly voted against the high annual budget of successive mayors and opposed the city's attempts to borrow more and more money through new bond issues and to obtain larger amounts in state aid. "The people of this state," he said, "should not bail out an extravagant and wasteful local administration."

When both our children, within the same year, married and left home to establish their own families, I felt bereft. But not Stanley—he knew the ties were strong. He was able to accept both Myron and Casey as adults, and consequently they were ready to turn to him when they needed advice or help. And no matter how busy Stanley was, their problems came first.

In 1942, when Myron was settled in Washington, he was offered a job with the Securities and Exchange Commission. The move entailed a number of difficulties: family, financial, future. Stanley gave a good deal of time and thought to the change, and finally wrote to Myron that "despite the domestic upset that is involved," in his own judgment the S. E. C. would be the wisest choice.

Myron made his move accordingly and, as it turned out, happily. It must have been hard on his wife, Skeeter, with their growing family, to uproot herself from New York, where she had spent her entire life, to go to Washington, then to Philadelphia, back to Washington and finally to White Plains. But apparently Skeeter was not one to be thrown—no matter where they landed, she managed to run a large household, bring up a quartet of

interesting, intelligent, happy children, and still find time
to be involved in community affairs. Stanley's satisfaction
in Myron's career was reinforced when he received this
letter from a fellow lawyer:

April 12, 1948

Dear Edith and Stanley:

I have just returned from a nine-day stay in Minne-
apolis, where I was on a utility-reorganization case in
which Myron was leading counsel for the Securities
and Exchange Commission. It was a very important
case, both from a public and an S. E. C. standpoint.
The amounts involved were large, and the case was
extremely complicated.

I thought you would be glad to know that Myron
handled this matter simply brilliantly. His argument
to the court took over four hours and was a master-
piece of presentation and advocacy. I cannot speak too
highly about it, so these words are not unduly enthusiastic. This represents not only my own views, but
the opinion of all of the lawyers (a flock of about a
dozen) who were interested in the matter.

Cordially yours,
Ralph Wolf

Myron's career has now taken him full circle; he is
associated with Stanley's family law firm—M. S. & I. S.
Isaacs.

Our daughter Casey, too, turned to Stanley with her problems. She had moved to Switzerland with her husband and son in 1956, when Snow was transferred to the Geneva seat of the International Labour Office. She found to her dismay that there was no local English-language newspaper in Switzerland from which American and British residents could learn the local news or business opportunities. She promptly set out to remedy the situation.

But the launching was difficult and frustrating, and she has since told me that she was ready to throw in the sponge if it hadn't been for the encouragement she got from her husband and from Stanley. One of Stanley's letters she treasured came after a year of struggling to get the *Weekly Tribune* running, and it gave her the necessary incentive to keep the paper going for the next six years, before she sold it to an American bidder:

> I was delighted to hear that you have been successful in putting that paper across. It is really a wonderful achievement even to get it started. I can realize the difficulties you faced, the obstacles that you had to overcome. We certainly hope that it will prove a highly profitable enterprise. In any event, no matter what its long-distance success or lack of success, you've done a remarkable job just to launch it . . .

It was exciting to us to find that the Swiss likewise recognized her achievement. A year after her newspaper made its debut we received a copy of *Annabelle*, a Swiss women's magazine, which had run a "profile" of Casey, designating her the "Genevoise of the Month."

Three years later Stanley and I climaxed a trip through Italy with a delightful week at the Herricks' in Geneva. Casey gave us a quick tour of her newspaper plant, and they arranged a cocktail party, where we could meet some of their friends. After we left, Stanley wrote to Casey of his pride and pleasure in their adjustment to a new life. This recognition from Stanley emphasized the wonderful relationship Casey had with him, despite the separation of time and space. Stanley always remained for both Myron and Casey—father, friend and idol.

❧ In 1942, when Dalton School was on the rocks, Stanley was appointed receiver. The financial mess he found there was incredible, despite the fact that Dalton had a "society" waiting list of hundreds of children.

It took drastic measures to straighten out their affairs, but Stanley managed it, and at the end of the housecleaning he was asked to stay on as a trustee and treasurer of the school. In addition to the usual duties of a treasurer, he handled all applications for scholarships, repairs of the building, and many problems concerning policy. It was through his influence that the school became thoroughly integrated, with Negro teachers as well as students. The scholastic standing was raised to the point where Dalton today is considered one of the finest schools in the country; and he put it on such a firm financial footing that he was able to establish a series of across-the-board salary raises only a few years after he became treasurer.

Stanley personally interviewed the parents of every child seeking a scholarship, and during the years that he served, he spent practically every Wednesday morning in the school.

William L. Shirer, a fellow member of Dalton School Board, once commented: "Like most great men loaded with responsibilities, Stanley was never in a hurry. You would have thought Dalton was his only interest in life." To all who had any knowledge of Stanley's activities, it did seem almost impossible for one man to accomplish all the things he did. I'm sure he couldn't have without his two most competent secretaries: Joan Hamlin, who knew the inner workings of City Hall, and Millicent Sturm, of whom he said, "I couldn't get along without Millicent. But the way she runs my law office, I think she could get along without me!"

BRIEF INTERLUDE

It was the weekend of my sixtieth birthday, and the family had come to Croton to help us celebrate. Sunday morning we played our usual game of tennis: Stanley and Casey against Myron and me. Stanley seemed to be trying harder but less effectively than usual, and we won. He looked hot and tired, and we decided to stop after one set. I'm sure he wasn't feeling well then. In the afternoon he didn't take his usual hike through the woods, which should have made me suspicious, but it didn't.

On Monday he took an early train to New York and spent two hectic days in his office. On Wednesday he looked and felt so ill that his secretary insisted he call his doctor. There a cardiogram told the story.

In those days we had no telephone in the cabin in Croton, and so the doctor phoned one of our neighbors, who gave me the message. Joji showed his tact and good sense by asking no questions, driving quickly, carefully. All he said was, "He be all right. We take care of him."

When a letter he had written to me Monday night eventually caught up with me, I understood the reasons for his heart attack.

June 19, 1944

Edith dear:

I've been going like sixty all day—your sixty, at full speed, no rest. Very rushed. It's seven and I'm still at the office.

Talked to Willkie, who approved my program.

Went over statement with Dennis Lynch who thought it over-long but otherwise liked it. Will get it ready by Wednesday for release Friday A.M.

Speaking over radio WNEW Thursday eve. 7:45 at request of Murray Davis, who will ask me questions on basis of the release, timed for A.M. newspapers next day.

Prepared speech for League of Women Voters (replacing LaGuardia) over WNYC Wednesday at 8:15.

Tonight two meetings plus work at home.

Tomorrow just as bad.

What do you mean I'm overworking? But I love you—young as you are.

He was a most impatient patient at the hospital. After only a week there he succeeded in persuading the doctors to let him go home, arguing that he would get just as good care there.

The usual treatment for heart attacks was six weeks of complete rest, with nursing care, pills, diet. Stanley got all but the complete rest. I wanted to have the telephone taken out of his room, but he wouldn't hear of it. His office, United Neighborhood Houses and sundry other organizations were in constant touch, his secretary came daily with batches of letters, and he dictated the answers forthwith. He saw relatives, friends, reporters, his associates at the M. S. & I. S. Isaacs law office, and Council members. To everyone who inquired, his answer was, "I feel fine."

His two greatest disappointments during this time were that he couldn't attend the Republican convention to work for Wendell Willkie's nomination (he had been elected a delegate) and that his sickness spoiled his 100 percent record of attendance at Council meetings.

At the end of the fifth week he was up and about. The doctor gave him strict instructions to take it easy, to avoid crowds, stairs, excitement of any kind, to take taxis. I tried scolding him, but without effect. Finally he sat me down and said, "Look, Edith, you can make an invalid of me, wrap me up in cotton wool, and maybe I'd live a year or two longer. But I wouldn't be happy. I'm doing the things I believe in—which I think are worthwhile, and the best way you can help me is to stop worrying."

I didn't stop worrying, but I did stop annoying him. Actually, he was right. Stanley lived for eighteen years after that first heart attack, and they were full, active, happy years for both of us.

✍ A year later, Stanley wrote to Dr. J. T. Salter in answer to his article on "Medals for Politicians." It is an eloquent expression of his lifelong political and personal philosophy.

April 3, 1945

Dr. J. T. Salter

Dear Dr. Salter:

. . . I have read your essay, "Medals for Politicians," and although I like it, I just cannot add any comment at the point you indicated. Frankly, I did not feel at all the "grief and anguish" that you ascribe to me. Of course I resented the fact that the rather vicious political forces opposed to me proved stronger than I could resist at the time. And I was sorry to have to give up an exciting job. Nevertheless, I have been able, thanks to the Proportional Representation system that we have in this city, to remain in public life, whether my enemies like it or not.

Further, I am rather thick-skinned on the whole, and was made angry rather than unhappy by what happened. I think, frankly, a man is of no use in public life if he takes that sort of thing personally or develops a "martyr complex." I agree wholly with what Theodore Roosevelt expressed in an address that I heard him deliver at Carnegie Hall in 1912. Near the end he said: "The leader, for the time being, is but an instrument to be used until broken and then to be cast aside; and if he is worth his salt he will care no more when he is broken than a soldier cares when he is sent where his life is forfeit in order that the victory may be won . . . The watchword for all of us is 'Spend and be spent!' "

I think he was absolutely right. Our job is to fight for what we believe in, win when we can, and if we are beaten, from time to time, start right over again; and not to retreat or to sulk.

I hope you won't think me pompous when I quote a verse which I understand, from the letters of William James, was inscribed over the mantel in his living room. As I recall it—I have not had time to check—it read: "A shipwrecked sailor, buried on this coast, bids thee set sail. Full many a gallant bark, when we were lost, weathered the gale."

In other words, my own attitude is to recover as fast as possible from defeat; if I can't come back personally, to help someone else to win out; and never to forget the importance of the cause and the very slight importance of the individual.

I am afraid that recognition comes to most public men only in the form of an obituary. But even in that form it helps to crystallize his influence—and, in a way, enables him to carry on after death itself . . .

Yours very sincerely,

Stanley M. Isaacs

WAR'S END

Ever since he was eight years old Joji had been an alien wherever he lived—in Argentina, in England, and in the United States. This, for a person as sensitive as Joji, was hard enough to bear, but when, in 1941, through no fault of his own, he was classed as an enemy alien, he really suffered.

I sympathized, for I knew how difficult it was for the

Japanese to get jobs during the war. Even Stanley objected to my employing Kawano (the first in my series of four Japanese servants) until he was assured that he carried a pink book—proof that he was under government surveillance.

When Joji came to us in 1944 he said, "Thirty years I live in America; every job I work hard; serve in Merchant Marine—*I'm* enemy alien? Oh yes, Uncle Sam say so. See, here is little pink book." And he showed it to us. It bore his photograph, his fingerprints, a record of his birthplace, and other identifying data. "Always I must carry it around like I'm a jailbird!" He shook his head sadly.

But in spite of this injustice, he definitely aligned himself with our side throughout the war. Strangely enough, the Japanese were "they." "Why they attack Pearl Harbor?" he would ask, or "How they think they can beat big country like United States?" The news of Hiroshima and Nagasaki shook him, but he finally accepted these as the necessary horrors of war. He comforted himself with "Perhaps war be over quicker now." And it was.

It was August 14, 1945; we were in Croton. Joji had raised a bumper crop of tomatoes and brought in a heaped-up basket that afternoon. These he planned to convert into tomato marmalade, one of Stanley's favorite confections. I always offered my assistance for these operations, knowing what his answer would be: "Don't need help, I fix myself."

I joined Stanley in the living room, where he was reading and listening to the radio at the same time. Suddenly there was a break in the program: "We interrupt this program for a special announcement. The war with Japan is over! Japan has accepted U. S. terms for peace!"

I rushed into the kitchen, followed by Stanley.

"The war's over, Joji! Our war with Japan!"

"War over? Is true, Mr. Isaacs?"

"Yes, Joji. We just heard it over the radio. Listen, it's on again."

I had never seen Joji cry before, but he stood there weeping, unashamed. Holding out his hand to us, he said, "I not your enemy, no more."

"You never have been," said Stanley.

"Now I celebrate. Yes? Hokay I leave marmalade for tomorrow?"

"Yes, of course," I said.

"How are you going to celebrate?" Stanley asked.

"Go New York. Perhaps get little drunk. Hokay I get little drunk? Not every day war is over."

"It's okay with me," I said.

"How about our going to New York too. There'll be lots of excitement," Stanley suggested.

"Let's," I said. "I'd love to."

We drove to the city with the radio going full blast. There wasn't much variation in the announcements, but Joji never tired of hearing the same thing. "You don't know what means, end of war. No enemy alien no more, no more little pink book, no more report every time I go for vacation—Atlantic City, Saratoga, Monmouth. Always I have to report—show little pink book."

"You did?" I asked.

"No, I don't do, but law say I should. Make me mad, so I don't do."

"Well, it's over now, Joji, you can forget it," said Stanley.

"Sure. Is why I celebrate."

And he celebrated. He tanked up at the nearest bar, then joined a couple of sailors on their way to Times Square. They boosted him up to the top of a lamppost, and when "The Star-Spangled Banner" came over a loudspeaker, Joji played an accompaniment on a tin horn. His antics were punctuated by frequent visits to bars. We didn't know how or when he got home, but he was asleep in his room when we went down for breakfast the next morning. I didn't wake him until five in the afternoon, when we were ready to go to Croton. He was not fit to handle the car, so I drove and he promptly fell asleep in the back seat.

It was almost dark when we reached the cabin. The first thing Joji saw was the basket of tomatoes he had picked the day before. "Now I make marmalade," he announced.

"You haven't time for that, Joji," I said. "It's late, and we're tired, and we want our dinner."

"Hokay, hokay, I cook dinner, marmalade, all same time."

I had long since learned that one didn't argue with Joji when he was like that. There was much clattering of dishes, pots and pans in the kitchen, followed by a loud crash. Presently Joji came into our room looking slightly crestfallen. "I have little accident," he announced. "Not too bad. Plenty more tomatoes in garden."

I never discovered exactly what happened, but all of our food that night tasted strangely of half-cooked tomato marmalade.

After dinner, tired, we went to bed.

Joji announced: "Now I sit on porch little while." Then, "Joji," said Joji, "you no enemy no more! Tomorrow we burn little pink book. Tomorrow we celebrate some more."

"You've done enough celebrating, Joji," Stanley called out.

"Hokay," he said, but a few minutes later we heard the unmistakable sounds of gurgling liquid, and a bottle landing heavily on a table. He had evidently brought an extra supply from the city. Suddenly he announced, "Now I sing 'Star-Spangled Banner.'"

It was just as well that he announced it, for I would have challenged anyone to recognize either the words or the tune. I have heard many singers, on key and off, warble our national anthem, but no other with the fervor and abandon of that midnight serenade.

"How long is this celebrating going to keep up?" Stanley asked. "I'd like to go to sleep."

"Joji," I called. "Go to bed. We want to sleep."

"Sure, sure. I think I sleep here. Is so peaceful." And he stretched out on a wooden porch bench. He kept repeating, "Is so peaceful!" at intervals, during which Stanley fell asleep and soon I too dropped off.

We were awakened by cries of "Fire! Fire! Help! Help!" It was Joji's voice. The room was fitfully lighted by a flickering ruddy glow. We rushed out to see the underbrush and small trees south of our house ablaze, and there was Joji, silhouetted against a wall of flame. He was shouting frantically as he played a hose on the fast-spreading fire. Stanley, clad in pajamas and moccasins, took command. He'd had experience fighting forest fires in Maine, and he quickly planned our strategy.

The hose no longer reached the fire, and flames were bursting out on three sides, so we collected every available pot and pail. It was my job to keep them filled, and Joji toted them to Stanley, who beat out the flames with a broom soaked in the water. In between my filling operations I had time to play the hose on the roof to prevent the flying sparks from setting fire to the house. And just to be on the safe side, I soaked the walls too, never noticing, until I went inside, that all the windows were open.

Stanley and Joji worked like fiends, and in less than an hour the fire was extinguished.

Stanley, poor darling, his face streaked with soot and sweat, his pajamas scorched and torn, dropped exhausted on the porch steps. "How on earth did this thing start?"

"Those picnickers who were here last week, remember, probably didn't put out their fires properly," I said, "and it's been working its way underground till it finally burst out."

"Maybe," said Stanley. "More likely a careless smoker threw a lighted match or cigarette into the woods."

Joji, looking pale and worn, was silent—obviously too tired to talk.

"Joji," I said, "you look sick. This has been too much for you, all those heavy pails. You were absolutely wonderful, wasn't he, Stanley?"

"He certainly was. I never saw anyone work so hard. You'd better go to bed, Joji, and have a good sleep."

"I don't sleep tonight," Joji answered.

"Why not?" I asked.

"Because—" A deep sigh.

"Because what?" I prompted.

"Because is my fault."

"What's your fault?" asked Stanley.

"Fire." Another deep sigh. "You know place where I burn rubbish, madame? Thousand times I build big bonfire that place, don't I? Nothing ever happen. Never have trouble. Tonight maybe wind blow little harder. Maybe fire is little bigger. Maybe—I'm little drunk."

"But why should you build a great big bonfire to-night? There was no garbage."

"I burn little pink book," he said.

LATTER YEARS

The latter years of Stanley's life were, in a way, the most fruitful. Although the Borough Presidency gave him the opportunity for concrete achievement, he was under constant fire as President because of his controversial stands.

Later he was thought of as the elder statesman of the city: "Mr. New York," as he was dubbed by the press.

He could almost do no wrong, and his advice and influence were sought on virtually any matter touching civic affairs. The reporters loved him and delighted in his irreverent treatment of the "inner circle." He was called on constantly to speak at meetings, dinners, on radio and television. And he thoroughly enjoyed his ever-busier, ever-varied schedule, turning over more and more of his private law practice, to which he had returned after the Borough Presidency, to his associates.

Stanley never tackled a job on the surface. Whatever he became involved in, he delved into—and added constantly to his grasp of practical matters. His work as treasurer of Dalton School included, among other things, complete charge of the upkeep of the buildings. This experience he put to good use in June, 1961, when the City Council received its yearly plea that ten million dollars be added to the Capital Budget for the modernization and reconstruction of schools. The State Commission on Investigation of School Buildings was already hard at work, investigating the deterioration of schools, when Stanley wrote Jacob Grumet, one of the commissioners. Stanley suggested that the reason the school situation was so desperate was that much of the money allotted for modernization had always been spent on ordinary repairs, such as the kind a superintendent would make in an apartment building. Such expenses had depleted the Capital Budget, when they should actually have been charged against the Expense Budget. As a corrective measure, Stanley proposed that the Board of

Education add to its payroll various mechanics—plumbers, plasterers, roofers, etc.—who could be shifted from school to school, making the necessary repairs. By this direct, less expensive method, ordinary repairs would be made quickly, bypassing the standard time-consuming steps of waiting for private contractors to make bids and then for both the Board of Education and the Board of Estimate to approve them. "I don't believe this idea has been considered by the Board of Education," Stanley said. "It would seem to me a constructive solution of their problem, except when genuinely extensive repairs and genuine modernization are involved."

Another very special interest of Stanley's was the day-care centers which were established in New York, largely through Stanley's own efforts, to care for children of working mothers.

And largely through his efforts they were continued. He often intervened in their behalf—for example, writing to MacNeil Mitchell in 1955, upon reading a bill that State Senator Mitchell supported, with strong backing in Albany. The bill, which seemed certain to be passed, would have rejected a number of requests from New York City—including day-care appropriation, as well as educational funds for handicapped and non-English-speaking students. Stanley drafted a strong letter of protest, saying the position was wrong on all three counts. "I am afraid that letter-writing means nothing," he admitted, and therefore always included in his letters practical solutions that would at least be considered. In this case, he suggested a meeting between the leaders of the Legislature and a delegation from New York City. Either that or a hearing on the bill when it was ready. The bill was not passed.

His door was always open to those who sought better services for children who were brought before the courts. He frequently consulted with Justine Polier and Sylvia Liese, two of our most dedicated judges in the family courts, as to how individualized care and greater community concern for neglected and deprived children could be achieved. He firmly resisted popular and even hysterical demands for harsh punishment as an answer to delinquency.

His concern for the welfare of the city's children did not stop there. The Citizens' Committee for Children of New York was one of the basic community organizations to which he contributed much of his time, as a board member and the chairman of its legislative section, working closely with Mrs. Eric Haight and Betty Bernstein. This enabled him to fight effectively in literally hundreds of cases touching the children of the city. He fought for free tuition at the city colleges, against the use of public funds for sectarian or discriminatory institutions, for increased state aid to the public schools.

In fact, the Brown-Isaacs bill of 1952 was the first law passed in the city of New York which barred city funds to child-care institutions that discriminated because of race, color or religion.

Stanley never let up in his fight against racial discrimination, which had begun as early as 1932, when his friend Francis Rivers was refused membership in the American Bar Association. Stanley protested that this was "un-American, unintelligent and unfair." Mr. Rivers, who already belonged to the Bar Association of the City of New York, was sponsored for membership in the national association by well-respected, influential lawyers. Under the circumstances—considering Mr. Rivers' own standing as a lawyer—the rejection came solely from the fact that he was a Negro. Writing to the president of the national organization, Stanley concluded: "I wonder if you realize what indignation such action causes . . ."

It was not until 1943 that Francis Rivers was admitted to the American Bar Association.

Sometimes, in his sensitivity to discrimination, Stanley saw wide significance in issues that seemed inconsequential, as in this letter to Freda Kirchwey:

Dear Freda:

I am always troubled by the word "national" in the phrase "Jewish National Homeland." I believe that Palestine should be open to immigration at once, but I have the general view that Dr. Magnus has often expressed, that its internal affairs must be worked out so that the Jews and Arabs participate with full equality in the handling of its affairs. I do not believe in a Jewish national state which would reduce anyone else, because of his race or creed, to the status of a minority without full rights, any more than I am ready to accept for Jews anywhere, or for Negroes anywhere, or for minority groups anywhere, a status within a country which gives them less by way of civil liberties and inherent rights than everyone else obtains. It is for that reason I would like to see the phrase "Jewish Homeland" used rather than "Jewish National Homeland," even though the Balfour Declaration makes use of the latter title—because it has been construed by so many to mean a Jewish national state in which nobody except Jews will be admitted to full citizenship . . .

Sincerely yours,

Stanley M. Isaacs

During his first campaign for the City Council, in 1941, his headquarters were in the Roosevelt Hotel. He had planned a luncheon for a group of his supporters and told the headwaiter that he was reserving a table for ten. "I want you to know that there are several Negroes in the group," he said.

"Oh, that's all right, Mr. Isaacs, we'll give you a private room."

"I don't want a private room, I want to be seated in the main dining room."

"But that's out of the question. We never seat Negroes in the main dining room."

"Very well," said Stanley, "you can tell the management that I am moving my headquarters from here tomorrow." It wasn't many minutes before the manager came scurrying in, and the luncheon was served in the main dining room.

In housing too he fought for equality, and in 1957 finally pushed through the Sharkey-Brown-Isaacs bill, which makes discrimination in housing—privately-owned as well as city-operated—illegal in New York City. But long before the passage of the bill he had fought to make its provisions a reality, protesting wherever he saw discrimination or a lack of foresight in preventing it. In 1943, when Stuyvesant Town was approved by the Board of Estimate without including a clause against racial discrimination, Stanley reacted immediately. "I can assure you that I have every intention of continuing the fight, and am by no means hopeless," he announced to a member of the Board. And he was right. Racial discrimination *was* prohibited in Stuyvesant Town.

His quarrel with discrimination in housing did not stop with the barring of tenants. On March 7, 1945, he wrote a letter to an influential realtor, Mr. Russel V. Cruikshank, noting that distinguished Negroes visiting friends in the city had been "grossly offended" by doormen or elevator operators. In general, such insulting behavior would not be approved by the owners, he said. And concluded: "It should be obvious that the tenants in an apartment have the right to determine their own visitors."

In another letter, to William Green, president of the A. F. of L., Stanley wrote: "I want to reinforce my request that you urge every international union which is part of your great organization to eliminate Jim Crow locals wherever they exist."

About labor he had much to say—and not just on the subject of discrimination:

May 10, 1957

Mr. August Heckscher, Director
The Twentieth Century Fund
New York, N. Y.

Dear Mr. Heckscher:

. . . I am a good deal troubled by the tendency toward what seems to me an unduly shortened work week—this, of course, may be a sign of old age. You prophesy that two decades hence the five-day work week is almost certain to have been reduced to four. Of course that *is* the tendency. It seems to me to reduce itself to the somewhat unsocial process of insisting upon making a satisfactory family living from part-time work.

I have been strong for the five-day week and the leisurely weekend, but I do not see any real advantage for anybody in a four-day work week, except in special areas like coal mining. It seems to me a stimulant to rising costs and more inflationary in its operation than the added cost of services which you describe as an important source of today's inflationary pressures.

I see the consequences, especially in the housing field. Housing labor has always been led by those who make every effort to shorten the work week, and in addition to produce only a carefully controlled amount of work during the actual hours of labor. The result has been an enormous increase in the cost of housing. It is utterly impossible to build new dwellings in a city like New York, and in our suburbs, within the price range of anyone but those far above the median level of income. This is partly due to the high cost of land, but it is mainly due to the high cost of the structure. In my opinion this is unhealthy for every-body—including the carefully restricted laborer him-self, who requires a cheaper end product.

I wonder whether we do have to accept this ten-dency without pointing out more emphatically the disadvantages from the point of view of inflation, and the fact that the product is priced considerably above those in greatest need of it? . . .

Sincerely yours,

Stanley M. Isaacs

He always had an eye for cutting expenses, even his own salary. Once again, in 1955, Stanley refused a raise:

September 2, 1955

Robert F. Wagner

Dear Mr. Mayor:

I understand that the Board of Estimate has voted an increased salary for both the Majority and Minority Leaders of the City Council.

For myself, as Minority Leader, I regard the salary that I have been receiving—namely, $9,500—ample compensation for the time that I am glad to devote to the work of the City Council.

Accordingly, I wish to advise you and the members of the Board of Estimate, that while I am appreciative of the consideration paid to the office of Minority Leader and the work that it entails, I shall not accept any increase in salary. I hereby request you to instruct the Budget Director to continue the line covering that office at the present rate of compensation.

I am compelled to add that I believe that the City just cannot afford the increases which are being voted so extensively in top salaries. In my opinion, they are based on a false premise. I do not believe that the City, in order to secure well-qualified executives, must compete on a salary basis with private industry. Those able citizens who would be glad to devote themselves to City services are not thinking just in terms of compensation. Like those who select the teaching profession or social service as a career, the very best qualified public servants will be found among those who are ready to accept an adequate but modest salary. There are far more attractive rewards for public service than an increased pay check. Very high pay, unfortunately, means keener competition from the *political* careerist, who may well be less qualified but more greedy of the opportunity, not to serve but to secure the emoluments of office . . .

Very sincerely,

Stanley M. Isaacs

Stanley's informative letters to the leaders of the New York Republican State Committee were useful in giving them ammunition for attacking the waste and extravagance of the Democratic administration. One instance of poor financing came in 1956, and Stanley blamed it on "fear on the part of the Mayor of antagonizing automobile owners." Governor Harriman seemed to favor a repeal of New York City's power to levy the automobile tax, which ranged from $5 to $10 per car owner and produced $9,000,000 of tax money every year. When the Mayor didn't protest, Stanley did. "Mayor Wagner has been cowardly about this and wants to get off the hook," he said. "He knows he needs the money but he does listen to the A.A.A." And such listening had already cost the city some $20,000,000 a year in revenues which would have been received by charging $5 a month to all automobile owners who parked their cars on the city streets; Stanley pointed out the double advantage in this plan, which would ease the parking problem as well as bring in money, and he contended that many garage owners took in more cars than they could handle and parked the overflow on the streets, with no benefit to the city. The Legislature had authorized the tax, but it had never been put into force.

Stanley uncovered numerous kinds of waste. In July 1957, writing to Ray Ghent, who was in charge of public relations for the Republican State Committee, he struck two blows at once: at the "incompetent wastrels" in the office of the Corporation Counsel and at the "wasteful and extravagant" plans for building the new School for Industrial Art. The office of the Corporation Counsel, which had been run so smoothly under Paul Windels, had painfully degenerated, said Stanley, and must be cleaned up. As for the school, under pretense of being economical, the planners had chosen one of the highest-priced sites in all of Manhattan. The plan also provided for a combination with an elementary school, that combination being already condemned both by the Public Education Association and by United Parents Associations.

Abuse of city regulations by people using legal loop-holes always got his back up. When an actress announced on the radio that she had managed to reach the studio by hiring an ambulance to the airport, Stanley was shocked. Instead of hailing a taxi, some people called an ambulance, and with all stoplights ignored, they rushed to make a takeoff. "This seems wrong to me," Stanley said simply, writing to Norman S. Goetz, of the Hospital Council. He asked whether Goetz would be interested in a bill requiring all private ambulances to be licensed by the license commissioner. But no law was passed, and even today, for a price, any healthy person can hire an ambulance.

Another cause for which he wrote and spoke and fought was freedom of speech—though he was active in fighting for any kind of freedom. In 1947, when he was unable to attend the "Save the Voice of Freedom" dinner, he wrote a long letter, to Dorothy Parker, leaving no doubts as to where he stood: "If 'we the people' who control our government are to be properly informed—if we are to exercise our suffrage only after full opportunity has been accorded us to form a sound opinion about the vital issues which confront us—we must have the right to hear those who entertain conflicting views, so that we may judge between them." With newspapers folding up or being absorbed by larger papers, the daily press could not discuss issues from *every* angle, as it should. On radio and in the press, Stanley said, there must be real and not "so-called" news—or the mythical iron curtain would operate here, in the United States.

Stanley was also active in the mental-health field and in the expedition of adoption proceedings, and he was able to push through many reforms. But no matter how deep his interest in any cause, he always recognized the dignity of his adversaries and their right to disagree.

Stanley was famous for his thoughtful letters of congratulations: on birthdays and other special events, even on the publication of an annual report. And he never failed to add a personal note:

May 9, 1955

Hon. Francis W. H. Adams

Dear Commissioner Adams:

Over the weekend I was able to read, with great interest, the annual report of the Police Department for the year 1954. I think you should know that you deserve sincere congratulations for the progress made during the year. Your administration, from my point of view at least, has been thoroughly sound; you have taken over full control of the Department; you are eliminating some conditions that required radical excision; and altogether the force has been greatly improved under your administration.

Most remarkable, however, is the fact that the report contains no handsome picture of the Commissioner. I know of no other City report these days that displays such modesty.

Faithfully yours,

Stanley M. Isaacs

Of the hundreds of letters Stanley received, asking for help in a variety of situations, none went unanswered. And often he not only acknowledged the problem but he found a solution:

June 16, 1954

Honorable Philip J. Cruise

Dear Mr. Cruise:

I received a very pathetic appeal from Mrs. Judy, now living at 226 Thompson Street, who tells me that she applied to the City Housing Authority on March 31, 1954, for an apartment but has heard nothing since that time.

Mrs. Judy tells me that her family numbers six people living in a four-room, cold-water flat. Her husband, her seventeen-year-old brother and she herself sleep in the living room. She expects a baby in October.

She tells me that her husband is a veteran, having spent three years in the Army, and has not too steady a job at the present time. I hope this does not mean that he is not eligible because of inadequate income—the other reasons presented are pretty powerful for replacing that overcrowded apartment with a decent home.

I respectfully ask that you investigate this application and see whether it comes within your sound categories. I hope that it does. As I have told you always, I am not asking you to waive any of your regulations but do believe this to be an urgent case that justifies prompt consideration.

> Very sincerely yours,
> Stanley M. Isaacs

Requests to speak at graduation exercises belonged to the category of appeals he couldn't refuse. But the most frequent pleas came from students who had to write papers on New York City government and needed Stanley's help. Children came to his office or to our house, and I listened in occasionally. He would spend an hour or more, answering all their questions, giving them an inspirational talk on the true meaning of citizenship, and read aloud a passage from Theodore Roosevelt's *Autobiography*. The last boy who came left starry-eyed, and a few weeks later, shocked to learn of Stanley's death, wrote me a touching letter of condolence, telling how much that visit had meant to him.

✍ John Lindsay and Stanley Isaacs became friends in the early fifties through their membership in the Young Republican Men's Club. They had the greatest respect and admiration for one another, and Stanley soon recognized John's potential. "John Lindsay is going places," he said to me. "He's the kind of independent thinker our party needs."

During each of the Lindsay congressional campaigns we had a house gathering of neighbors to meet the candidate. Stanley presided at the first two, and I carried on the tradition, after his death in 1962, at the next two. Joji welcomed all the guests, proud to add Lindsay to our family circle.

One afternoon in October '65 during the mayoral campaign Joji came home in great excitement: "Who you think I meet in Madison Avenue?" And without waiting for my answer: "Mr. Lindsay. He was going round making speeches, and I ask him, 'You want I should take you to all bars round here? You meet lots of people that way.' He say, 'Sure!' So I take him to all three bars where they know me. Then he make little speech, shake hands with everybody, and everybody like him and clap when he go out."

On election night I was at the Lindsay headquarters, listening to the returns with his family and friends. Things looked bad around eleven o'clock and I went home feeling blue.

Joji greeted me with an excited "Lindsay ahead! Lindsay ahead!" We anxiously watched the television together, and finally, soon after midnight, it was clear that Lindsay had won. Laughing and excited, we drank a toast to the new Mayor.

Then Joji announced, "I go now."

"At this hour!" I cried. "Why are you going out?"

"I go to my three bars. I thank my friends for making my Mr. Lindsay Mayor."

STANLEY, THE SUNG HERO

Despite Stanley's natural humility and his myriad acts of kindness that went unknown, recognition still came from all sides and in many forms. Much of the wall space in our house on East 96th Street which is not hidden by books is now covered with awards for civic, humanitarian and educational services.

The following is a fair sample:

THE CITIZENS UNION OF THE CITY OF NEW YORK

presents

THE WILLIAM JAY SCHIEFFELIN AWARD

FOR DISTINGUISHED PUBLIC SERVICE

to

STANLEY M. ISAACS

As Borough President of Manhattan, as Councilman and Minority Leader of the City Council and as President for over twenty-five years of United Neighborhood Houses, Stanley Isaacs has set an inspiring example of civic conscience in action. He has been in the forefront of every battle for civil liberties, fair play for minority groups, decent standards of public welfare and better housing and recreation. A courageous and fair fighter for what he believes to be right, he has won the admiration and respect of opponents as well as friends. The cause has always been more important to him than personal aggrandizement and he has often worked quietly and effectively, letting others take the bows. For this as well as other reasons, it is an especial pleasure to present him with this testimonial to our respect and affection.

At the Citizens Union 61st Annual Dinner,
Biltmore Hotel, May 5, 1958

> Milton M. Bergerman
> Chairman

> George H. Hallett, Jr.
> Executive Secretary

Three of the honors that he valued the most came to him during the last few months of his life: the Theodore Roosevelt medal for distinguished service, the degree of Doctor of Humane Letters from the Hebrew Union College, and his election to membership in the Century Club.

Other tributes, less formal, were legion. We are a family of rhymesters, and many of our friends are similarly addicted. There was rarely an occasion of any importance, such as a special birthday, a dinner in Stanley's honor (and there were many of these) or the winning of an election (and Stanley, who ran for office eight times, never lost) that did not produce a rash of rhymes, songs or skits.

The practice began with our wedding, for which our friends published a special newspaper full of amusing songs, news items, editorials and a "personals" column. The next special event was our tenth wedding anniversary, for which our family and friends gave a surprise party, differing from such celebrations in that we were really surprised. They staged an elaborate performance called "Gilbert, Sullivan and Isaacs," with a libretto and songs composed by George S. Kaufman, Arthur Guiterman and others.

When United Neighborhood Houses gave a dinner in Stanley's honor, there were the usual laudatory speeches —too many and too long. When it was Stanley's turn to reply, he rose and said, "I thank you all. I too have prepared a speech"—he held it up and tossed it aside— "but it's midnight. Cinderella knew when it was time to go home, and so do I." There was thunderous applause.

For his seventieth birthday, in 1952, we all joined in producing a special edition of *The New Yorker*, with Stanley's face on the cover. Every department was ingeniously parodied by such clever writers as Melville Cane, Newman Levy, Anita Despres, Babbie Langsdorf, Helen Kaufmann and Sophie Goldsmith.

Our Casey wrote:

Let others sing of Stanley
The honest politician,
Who does what he believes in
Despite the opposition

> *But I sing of Daddy because*
> *I remember when he carried*
> *me on his back, on hikes . . .*

The man the people choose
To voice their views is Stanley;
They say he's upright, liberal,
And not Republicanly

> *But I choose Daddy because*
> *he wrote me such wonderful*
> *letters . . .*

Then there's the Stanley Isaacs
Who's on the old school team
When Dalton School was in the red
Made black their color scheme

> *But Daddy's the man who*
> *really taught me to love*
> *books . . .*

Stanley Isaacs is the man
Against discrimination;
He gives us public housing,
Good health and education

> *But Daddy gave me wonder-*
> *ful private housing to grow*
> *up in . . .*

Stanley Isaacs is a man
Unable to offend,
The only politician
Politicians call a friend

> *But I love Daddy because despite everyone's claims on him, his time and his energy, he still always managed to be Daddy*

Myron wrote one too, which began:

A day to remember
Is the first Tuesday after the first Monday in November,
One of the great American propaganda dates,
Especially for candidates.
Whether you like Ike, or are madly for Adlai,
I recommend to your attention a man whom you can endorse,
Without ever apologizing or feeling badlai.

And ended:

A man who hath an affinity
For attractive femininity,
But needeth
Only Edith;
A man who devotes most of his life to the foible
Of making other people's lives more enjoible;
A man who at the moment ain't runnin for nuttin,
But whenever Stanley M. Isaacs runs for any office whatsoever,
I'll wear his campaign button.

In 1954, for no special occasion, Adele Levy, president of the Citizens' Committee for Children, decided that a dinner should be given in Stanley's honor, and proceeded to organize it. The grand ballroom and adjoining rooms and corridors of the Biltmore Hotel were jammed with Stanley's friends. It was a beautiful party, with only a few speeches, none too long, and songs (natch) by Casey, Myron and me. The grand finale was a delightful Ogden Nashian poem written and read by Elly Guggenheimer, illustrated by slides of most amusing photographs of Stanley at all ages engaged in all manner of pursuits. The following is a greatly abridged version:

Ladies and Gentlemen—at dinners of this type it is the
*   custom*
To make speeches about the guest of honor until you have
*   completely embarrassed and*
*   fussed 'em,*
And to have all the speeches lengthy—and a good part
*   of an houry*
And flowery,
And trite,
And to point out that the guest of honor works
*   thirty-six hours a*
*   day doing what is right,*
And to announce in tones that are properly fervent
That he's a devoted public servant.
Now in case you think what we are about to say tonight
*   will be different, don't;*
It won't.
The only thing that will be new
Is that it's true.
Because our guest of honor is always right and a
*   public servant and*
*   a super friend,*
And he does good works without end,
In such numbers that if we listed them you'd think
*   we were deceiving,*
And so we figured seeing is believing.
We present therefore something which, for want of a

better word, we are
calling "Portraits of
a Gentleman,"
Which is inadequate because he is a phenomenal combination
of a moral, ethical, physical and mental man.

For instance, his ethics are so ethical that no breath of
scandal can ever find him,
And his physique is so physical that anyone who starts
walking with him ends up two blocks
behind him,
And his morals have been ever so moral all his life,
According to his wife,
All of which we will illustrate by portraits which you
are about to see,
Which were put together at great time, trouble and expense,
by his family, friends, the committee and me.

.   .   .

Well, we told you when we started that we think our guest
of honor would be voted
Of all guests of honor for the last seventy-two years the
most distinguished and devoted,
Not just for the jobs he does, the number of which is
incredible,
Or for the public dinners which he eats, most of which
are inedible,
Or for his integrity, which would have astonished Diogenes,
Or for his family—both ancestors and progenies,
Or for the people he's helped and the friends he has made,
Or for being always unafraid,
Or for his public career, which is a monument anyone would
be proud about,
Or for all the good causes he has stood for and fought for
and shouted loud about.
The reason there is no guest of honor we would put
above him
Is—we love him.

Our golden wedding anniversary was a gala affair to which we invited three hundred and sixty of our "most intimate friends." The songs and skits written for the occasion filled a thirty-page souvenir volume.

Then there was the dinner given in Stanley's honor by the Republican Club of his district, at which Governor Rockefeller, Senator Javits, Congressman Lindsay and other Republican dignitaries spoke—and more "orchids" were handed out.

In 1962 a thing unheard of in politics happened: Stanley's political "opponents" (I put the word in quotes because the very fact belies it) in the New York City Council, of which Stanley was the minority leader, gave a dinner in his honor. It was a beautiful affair, outdoors at The Tavern-on-the-Green in Central Park, with all the Council and most of their wives present. The president of the Council and the majority leader were the chief speakers, and each member paid tribute to the man whose ability and courage they respected, and whose warmth and friendliness they loved.

The majority leader said, almost sadly, "You know, Stanley, ninety-five percent of the time you're not fighting us, you're teaching us, leading us, you're inspiring us, but it's the five percent that always gets into the papers."

Stanley laughed. "That's the only way I can make the papers," he said.

The grand climax was the presentation of a handsome desk set engraved "To Stanley M. Isaacs, with the affection and esteem of his colleagues on the New York City Council."

Stanley was deeply moved. "These tributes," he said, "coming from you, the opposition, mean more to me than you can guess."

One of his great admirers was Judge Learned Hand, who wrote to him on many subjects. This was the letter I prize above all:

Dear Stanley:

I have received a good many letters since my retirement, but none have given me greater gratification than yours. I think I need not tell you how much I have admired your public career, especially the incorruptible courage with which you faced abuse and misunderstanding. If I could see among our public officers anything approaching prevalence of such qualities as you have always brought to your duties, I should have a much more robust confidence in our final emergence from the deep dangers we are in.

Sincerely,

Learned Hand

*　*　*

The end came suddenly. Early on Monday, July 9, 1962, he had his breakfast on the porch at Croton just outside my open window. We talked about our plans for the week and the weekend. He asked if I'd want to go to the Shakespeare-in-the-Park play on Thursday. I wasn't sure, said I'd let him know. When he was ready to leave he kissed me goodbye.

We called each other several times Monday, Tuesday and Wednesday. I had decided not to go to Shakespeare in the Park but wanted to go in Wednesday to visit my brother, who was to have a cataract operation. Stanley dissuaded me, saying that he would phone the hospital Wednesday, visit my brother Thursday and keep me informed. The last call came at about eight-thirty Wednesday evening, just to say goodnight.

At four A.M. I was awakened by our dog's barking and the sound of voices. I turned on my light and saw Myron and Joji standing in the doorway—both looking pale and shaken.

Myron put his arms around me.

Somehow I knew what had happened.

"Stanley!" I said.

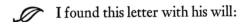 I found this letter with his will:

June 18, 1946

Edith dear:

Ever since June 1944, I've known that I may die at any time and without warning. I have no fear at all of this—I've lived gladly, and if death comes, I'll lay me down with a will. I'm leaving little by way of possessions—but I've tried to be true to my stock, as TR said to Myron. I've worked as hard as I could, and without letdown to make some contribution to those around me—to live honestly, fight hypocrisy and fraud and dishonesty and appeasement of dangerous forces to the best of my ability.

This you should know; and I'm writing this letter on your birthday to tell you. You've helped me beyond measure and at all times; you've urged me on and never minded the sacrifices which you shared. No one could have been as wonderful to me—no one else as loyal and sweet at all times. You've made an endless number of friends for both of us. I love you dearly— and when I die, if I can't express myself, I want you to know you'll be in my mind—my last thoughts will be of you.

Stanley

Although recognition came to Stanley before his death, his obituaries served to point up how much his life had meant to so many. The city was in mourning: the expressions of loss and shock poured in—personal messages of sympathy by the thousands. Entire pages of newspapers were devoted to his life and death, and announcements were made over the radio at half-hour intervals all day long.

It is hard to choose among the many tributes he received, but it seems to me that the first few paragraphs from the New York *Herald Tribune* best sum up the feelings of Stanley's city:

July 13, 1962

At 12:15 A.M. yesterday, when Stanley M. Isaacs died, New York City politics lost its voice of constructive opposition.

Accolades came from everywhere during the day. Democratic City Hall ordered the flag flown at half-staff in memory of its Republican critic.

And today important people will assemble for the funeral service at noon at Congregation Shaaray Tefila presided over a century ago by Mr. Isaacs' grandfather Rabbi Samuel Isaacs.

Mr. Isaacs' official title was modest: Minority Leader of the City Council. The apogee of his political career was long past. Twenty-one years ago his stubborn independence cost him the Manhattan Borough Presidency and the chance to run for Mayor someday.

It was his unofficial credentials that made Stanley Myer Isaacs at the age of 79 a landmark of prominence in this city of many human landmarks.

He personified responsible opposition in a city that rarely rewards opposition. He symbolized the spirit of reform although reform loses far more often than it wins. He epitomized courtliness in public office in a community where politics is often a haven for the boorish. He was a real-estate man who fought health hazards and racial discrimination in housing.

Above all he was a vivid personality who participated in almost every do-good activity imaginable, who often found himself a minority even within his minority party, who never let party loyalty or personal convenience stand in the way of a good fight.

The *Herald Tribune* called Stanley Mr. New York. To the *Times* he was a Warrior for the People. To me, he was all that, and much more.

ABOUT THE AUTHOR

EDITH S. ISAACS was born and educated in New York City and graduated from Barnard College with honors. Whenever Stanley Isaacs ran for office during the last twenty-five years of their fifty-two years of marriage, Mrs. Isaacs was her husband's campaign manager.

For the past twenty-five years Mrs. Isaacs has served on the Board of the Women's City Club of New York; she is the Honorary Chairman of the Stanley M. Isaacs Neighborhood Center and serves on the boards of several other charitable organizations.

Although Mrs. Isaacs is an inveterate writer of stories, plays and jingles, this is her first full-length book.